D0961874

BETTY
A GLAD AWAKENING

Also by Betty Ford

THE TIMES OF MY LIFE

BETTY
A GLAD AWAKENING

Betty Ford
with CHRIS CHASE

DOUBLEDAY & COMPANY, INC.
GARDEN CITY, NEW YORK
1987

*Unless otherwise credited, photographs
are part of Betty Ford's private collection
and are used with permission.*

Grateful acknowledgment is made for permission to reprint the following:

Excerpt from "The Labyrinth" by W. H. Auden, copyright 1945, renewed 1973 by W. H. Auden, is reprinted from *W. H. Auden: Collected Poems*, edited by Edward Mendelson (New York: Random House, Inc.), by permission of Random House, Inc., and Faber and Faber, Ltd.

Excerpt from *The Family Reunion* by T. S. Eliot, copyright 1939 by T. S. Eliot, renewed 1967 by Esme Valerie Eliot, is reprinted by permission of Harcourt Brace Jovanovich, Inc., and Faber and Faber, Ltd.

Excerpt from "An Epilogue" by John Masefield is reprinted from *Selected Poems of John Masefield*, with preface by John Betjeman (New York: Macmillan, 1978), by permission of Macmillan Publishing Company and the Society of Authors, London, as literary representative of the estate of John Masefield.

Excerpt from "Renascence" by Edna St. Vincent Millay. From *Collected Poems*, Harper & Row. Copyright 1912, 1940 by Edna St. Vincent Millay. Reprinted by permission.

Excerpt from *A Few Days*, copyright © 1985 by James Schuyler (New York: Random House, Inc., 1985), is reprinted by permission of Random House, Inc.

Excerpt from "Pursuit" by Robert Penn Warren, copyright 1942 by Robert Penn Warren, is reprinted from *Selected Poems 1923–1975* (New York: Random House, Inc.) by permission of Random House, Inc.

Designed by Wilma Robin

Library of Congress Cataloging-in-Publication Data
Ford, Betty, 1918–
Betty, a glad awakening.
1. Ford, Betty, 1918–   . 2. Presidents—United
States—Wives—Biography. 3. Alcoholics—United States—
Biography. 4. Ford, Gerald R., 1913–   —Family.
I. Chase, Chris. II. Title.
E867.F657   1987   973.925′092′4 [B]   86–19646
ISBN 0-385-23502-X

With gratitude and love to my family,
who were there when I needed them.

ACKNOWLEDGMENTS

I want to thank all my friends, especially those who contributed so much to this book: Leonard and Nicky Firestone, Meri Bell and Dell Sharbutt, Pat Benedict, Clara Powell, Muriel Zink, Dolores and Bob Hope, Ed and Helen Johnsen, John and Joan Sinn, Bob Barrett, Sheika Gramshammer, Jim and Joan Kemper, Paul and Mary Jane Jenkins and Wallis Annenberg.

I want to thank the many groups who have shared with me in my recovery: the women from Laguna Beach who were there in the beginning, the members of the Eisenhower Medical Center Auxiliary who help us at the Betty Ford Center and also with the Alcohol Awareness Hour and also, those special friends from the Coachella Valley, Denver and Vail.

I want to thank the physicians, clergymen and others who, working in the field of alcoholism and drug addiction, helped me to understand this disease. Among them are Dan Anderson, Vern Johnson, Joe Cruse, Joe Pursch, LaClaire Bissell, Father Joe Martin, Sheila Blume, Stan Gitlow, Max Schneider, Bob Niven, Ian MacDonald, Stephanie Covington and Joe Takamine.

I want to thank the Board of Directors of the Betty Ford Center, John Schwarzlose, our executive director, Jim West, our medical director, and all of our able and dedicated staff at the Betty Ford Center.

And special thanks to John Sinn, President of Eisenhower Medical Center. Throughout the years, he has been my strong advisor, always available and willing.

I want to thank Chris Chase, whose talent and patience allowed us to collaborate so effectively.

Additional thanks go to Loretta Barrett of Doubleday, whose encouragement and enthusiasm convinced me the time was right for this book.

I want to thank Ann Cullen, my assistant. She has provided a sounding board, she has shared with me good, bad and indifferent moments and has been like a member of my family and, most of all, she is my friend.

I want to thank my brother, Bill Bloomer, and his wife, Betty, for helping me know how pleasant it is to share memories with a sibling.

And once again, I want to thank my family—Jerry, Mike and Gayle, Jack, Steve, Susan and Chuck—for their love.

AUTHORS' NOTE

Where names of real people have been used, those people have given us permission.

All other individuals are composites. Physical characteristics, and details of the stories of doctors, nurses, patients, patients' families and friends at Long Beach, the Betty Ford Center, group meetings, etc., have been altered in order to protect their privacy.

But in this world another hope keeps springing
In an unexpected place . . .

        T. S. Eliot, *The Family Reunion*

When I was in treatment at Long Beach, the naval hospital where I went to get clean and sober, I was required to write what they called an autobiography—a few pages was all the therapists wanted—detailing where I had gone off the track.

I could not do it.

I suppose I was so wrapped up in the image I had been presenting to the public that I didn't see anything wrong with my life. I was married to the perfect man, I had four perfect children, I had a new house and, after thirty years of married life, all new furniture. As far as I was concerned, everything was going along just fine, and I didn't know why these therapists should be suggesting anything different.

It seems quite clear now that I did not want to open the closet door, and have everything tumble out. You can't deal with everything coming at you all at once. You're afraid you'll be overwhelmed, maybe drink or use again, maybe even take your own life in your desperation to escape.

You know something's wrong, but you say it's all fine. My friend Muriel Zink describes this as "honest self-deception."

You face what you're able to face, and more is revealed to you when you can handle the revelations.

In Long Beach, I couldn't handle much, and certainly I could not write the truth.

Now here I am embarking on a different kind of autobiography, and I'm not sure I can write this one either.

"What is she *talking* about?" you're saying. "She *wrote* one autobiography, didn't she?"

Yes, she did. Let me explain. *The Times of My Life*, published after my husband and I left the White House, was not—except for one chapter added at the last minute—about my drinking or my pill taking. There was a lot of "honest self-deception" in it, though there was a lot of truth too. But basically, it was the story of a girl from Grand Rapids, Michigan, and her marriage to a man who later became the thirty-eighth President of the United States.

I know more about that girl now, and I know what I want to do with this new book. And what I don't want to do. I don't want to write what we alcoholics call war stories. Testimonials to the horrors of drinking. You listen to some of them, and you think: My God, if my life was like that, I'd drink too.

This book is going to be about recovery, mine and other people's. And how recovery works and how sometimes it doesn't. I would like it to be funny, not sad, and I would like anyone who reads it to understand that while I know something about alcoholism, I am no authority on the subject. I can't tell anyone how to get well. I can only carry the message about how it was for me, and the things that helped *me* to get well.

At first, I wasn't willing to share these things except in groups of other alcoholics. The idea of leaping into print bothered me. I have a husband who supports me, and I didn't choose to make money out of my recovery. That would be counterproductive to the program I live by, a program that says, if you want to keep it, you have to give it away.

Then I realized that was no problem. I give away the fees I'm paid for making speeches about alcohol and drug addiction— they go to help support the Betty Ford Center and other treatment centers—and I could do the same with any monies from a book.

What was more, a book could reach so much further than my voice in a speech, or my words in a letter.

At Long Beach, I got sacks of letters asking for help. This

person had lost his faith, that one had been brought down by drugs, alcohol, depression, illness.

At the time, I didn't know how to answer them. I had to get home before I could write and say, see your clergyman, go to your local council on drugs and alcohol, find a support group.

It was general advice, and there was nothing wrong with it. But what I didn't understand then, and do understand now, is that there is joy in recovery, and in helping others discover that joy.

Sometimes I'm asked if I feel I have a mission. I don't. I'm not that presumptuous. I don't think God looked down and said, "Here's Betty Bloomer, we're going to use her to sober up alcoholics." But I do think people relate to someone who has the same problems they have, and who overcomes them. And I think God has allowed me—along with thousands of others—to carry a message, a message that says, there's help out there, and you too can be a survivor. Look at us. Look at me.

Since my survival has often depended on others, there will be other voices heard here. I am going to turn to family and friends for help in reconstructing this journey of recovery. Some of them saw me more clearly than I saw myself, and all of them loved me until I could love myself.

And, through and over everything,
A sense of glad awakening.
Edna St. Vincent Millay

BETTY
A GLAD AWAKENING

1

> I will lift up mine eyes unto the hills,
> from whence cometh my help.
>
> Psalms 121

There are mountains all around the Betty Ford Center, blue-gray in the distance, massive and enduring. Once in a while even a patient who doesn't believe in God will admit that if you look at those mountains long enough, you start to suspect there's something out there greater than you, you're filled with a sense of wonder.

Wonder is what I was feeling on October 3, 1982, the day we dedicated the Betty Ford Center.

There was the 15th Air Force Band from March Air Force Base, and the U.S. Army Chorale, and a tent for the invited guests. It was a huge tent that held four hundred people. And the sun was shining, and there were buildings waiting for our first patients, and all I could think was, three recovering alcoholics did this. Joe Cruse, Leonard Firestone and Betty Ford built this out of Joe's dream, and a patch of desert.

We didn't do it alone, but we did it.

I took a lot of teasing on Dedication Day.

When Leonard Firestone got up from his seat on the dais to make his little speech, he accused me of being a slave driver. "I remember early on," he said, "she called me about every day.

'Have you done this? Have you done that? Have you followed up on this?' And I think it may have been after the second or third call one day, I said, 'Dammit, Betty, I'm doing the best I can.' I thought that might get her off me, but it didn't."

Then Leonard turned to Jerry. "Mr. President," he said, "you're damn lucky you're not an alcoholic!"

Vice President George Bush razzed me too. He said my assistant had told him I was a busybody, and that "not long ago, when this building was still a skeleton of girders and beams, she saw Betty out here thrashing around wearing a hard hat, and if that day Betty had not only inspected the place, but tightened a few bolts and welded three or four joints, no one would have been the least bit surprised."

I guess it's okay, as long as he didn't say *smoked* a few joints. After all, we're talking about a rehab center.

Bob Hope stood there in front of the very patrons and benefactors I'd been soliciting for cash, and accused me of having had my hands out "palms up for the last two years. . . . She's extracted so much money from people around here that next year she's going to be poster girl for the IRS."

In her speech, Dolores Hope, chairman of the board of Eisenhower Medical Center (the Betty Ford Center is a corporate part of Eisenhower), was not respectful either. But she pronounced herself impressed. "I did not see this facility until today," Dolores said, "and I can't believe anything this good could have been done without me."

My husband wasn't funny. My husband, who, when I told him he would be very important in this book, said, "No, I'm just a minor character," told the audience that he was speaking for our kids and our grandchildren as well as himself. He said, "We're proud of you, Mom . . . we want you to know that we love you." And when he talked about my recovery, he broke. He'd only done that in public one other time, after my mastectomy, as he'd faced the press and said I was okay, that I would be okay.

Ask people who were there what they remember best about the Dedication of the Betty Ford Center, and most of them say Jerry.

2

"Your dear little husband cried," Dolores Hope says, ignoring the fact that my dear little husband is over six feet tall. "His dear little eyes filled up, and oh, God, it really knocked us out. It was beautiful, and we went to the Dedication dinner, and talked about it."

My son Steve says, "My strongest memory of the day is how proud Dad was when he got up there. He talked about you, and he fought back tears, and I just saw the love between you."

Steve remembers that I looked loving, John Sinn, President of the Board of Eisenhower Medical Center, remembers that I looked anxious. They are both right. John Schwarzlose, the executive director for the Center, reminds me that I sat on the dais between Dolores Hope and George Bush, "and everybody was watching you, and twice, President Ford started to choke up when he was talking. I don't think most people were aware of how much the day meant to him because it meant so much to you."

Joe Pursch (the doctor in charge of Long Beach during my stay there) agrees that many listening to Jerry "felt a tug at the throat." Dr. Pursch says he was also touched by the miracle that "this thing was really happening." He compares helping alcoholics to delivering babies. "A baby is trapped in the mother's body, very isolated, and an alcoholic who is still drinking is imprisoned in kind of the same way—in the apartment, lights low, phone off the hook, television on, but not watching, cigarette in one hand, drink in the other, and that's the whole world. In either case, delivering a baby, or helping an alcoholic stop drinking, you're in at the creation of a new life."

Dr. Pursch saw the Dedication as a portent of marvels to come. "The media were there," he says. "The Vice President of the United States was there, so it was all out in the open, it was laying the foundation for a place that would deliver many babies."

Our friend Ed Johnsen, a builder who's on our board of directors, says for him, also, Jerry's speech was "the most significant. He just stood there and offered a tribute from the heart."

Meri Bell Sharbutt, my teacher and guide since Long Beach

—she is thirty years sober—was experiencing mixed emotions. "I saw the first slabs of cement in this thing," she says. "I saw the first plans when it had no name, it was just a vision of Joe Cruse. And then you got well, recovered, and you gave your permission to call it the Betty Ford Center. And I sat there at the Dedication wondering: Are you strong enough to withstand the onslaughts of people from every side? People who would be thinking of the Betty Ford Center as an extension of your sobriety? Or as an aggrandizement of your sobriety?"

Meri Bell knows the dangers of arrogance. A priest once said, "Meri Bell has humility, and she's proud of it," and Meri Bell says that, for six months, she thought that was a compliment.

It's even worse when you're in the public eye. People crowd around you and ask for advice and tell you you're wonderful, and you can easily build up a false sense of your own importance. Which is why, at Long Beach, Joe Pursch had put me in a room with three other patients, instead of giving me the private room I'd demanded. Right off, he was telling me, hey, lady, you may have been the wife of a President, but in here, you're nothing special.

My son Jack says the Dedication was less of a high to him than to "some of the people there who had been involved with the project. Because to me, the real victory was what had happened with Mother."

For several of my colleagues at the Center, the Dedication wasn't such a big deal either. Our opening, next morning, was what they were pointed toward.

"The staff was geared up, looking forward to Monday, and the first patients arriving," John Schwarzlose says. "So for us, it was like, well, it's an honor to be at the Dedication, but just wait till tomorrow."

Dr. Joseph Cruse, our founding medical director, says he was thinking that "we'd come a long way. The actual floor plans for the Betty Ford Center are from some slides I made in 1966, when I wanted to build a cancer hospital where the families could live with the patient. And I came to California drinking, with this dream.

"For somebody who had wandered up and down Wilshire Boulevard with a hip flask in one pocket and a letter from President Eisenhower in the other (the letter said what a good idea a live-in cancer hospital was), trying to raise money and drinking every night, this was quite a culmination."

For me, too.

Good Morning America was there, shooting a special segment, and my assistant, my right arm, Ann Cullen, was standing at the back of the tent with David Hartman's producer, pointing out notables. "That's so-and-so, you might want to talk to him. Or her. Or them."

Of my children, only Jack and Steve, the California contingent, came to the Dedication. The two from the East didn't make it, they didn't want to travel so far just to take part in a packed-with-people weekend. They won't come when we have a golf tournament either, because we're too busy running the tournament to talk to them. Susan and Mike said they'd visit when the Dedication was over, and we'd have more time together.

More time. It's a family joke. Jerry and I used to drive past when they were building the Betty Ford Center, and I'd say, "I'll be so glad when we get it up and open, because then I'll be free."

I couldn't imagine how seductive the Center would be for me, how much of my life it would take over.

At the Dedication, I had to speak, and I was scared. George Bush introduced me, and I tried to say a little about how I had felt coming home after treatment to the desert, to the serenity of these mountains that I loved. And I thanked everyone who had given us donations, or supported us in any way that had made the Center a reality. And I explained to the audience that one of the problems of alcoholics is that they tend to be perfectionists.

"The other day," I said, "I came over here to check, in my perfectionist way, on the last-minute details. Were the windows clean? Was everything in place? And as I walked up the path, I noticed that, thanks to all the water, fertilizer, peat moss and seed we'd put around, the grass was beginning to come up. You can see a wonderful green haze out there, it sort of looks like the stubble of a new beard, but it's beautiful. And I couldn't help but think, this was a pile of sand, and we've made it come alive. And it's going to be even more alive, because people will come here for help; there is going to be a way for them, a new life."

Later, after the music, the speeches, the congratulations were over, people drifted out onto the campus. At one point, Leonard and I were standing there, and we looked out across the still raw landscape. We had been through so much together, traveling the country pleading for money, fighting for new legislation, trying to foist off the presidency of the place—"You do it!" "No, you do it!"—on each other, and we had come so far.

The basic buildings were up, the trees were planted, we had assembled what we thought was the finest staff a rehabilitation center had ever put together, and they were all set to go. I said to Leonard, "Can you *believe* this?" and he said, "Hell, no, I really can't." And we laughed, and then we cried. For happiness.

And I thought about a morning four years earlier when I had cried for shame, out of weakness and fear. I was dying, and everyone knew it but me.

6

2

In the middle of the journey of our life
I came to myself in a dark wood where
the straight way was lost.

Dante Alighieri

April 1, 1978. We had been in our new California house just two weeks. I sat on the green-and-white couch in the living room, my husband's arm around me, and I cried. I didn't say a word, just listened, and cried.

We were having an intervention, starring me. My husband, my children, two doctors, a nurse and a couple of friends had gathered to tell me they were concerned about my failing health, and thought I had a problem with alcohol and drugs.

I'd never heard of an intervention, and I would just as soon have kept it that way. I didn't want to hear *any* of what my family was telling me.

My makeup wasn't smeared, I wasn't disheveled, I behaved politely, and I never finished off a bottle, so how could I be alcoholic? And I wasn't on heroin or cocaine, the medicines I took —the sleeping pills, the pain pills, the relaxer pills, the pills to counteract the side effects of other pills—had been prescribed by doctors, so how could I be a drug addict?

I had done everything in my power for my husband and our four kids I had loved so much. I had done everything in my power to help my husband's career. In my own mind, at least, I had always been there for them, and I truly believed I had given a hundred percent. My mother's voice was always in my ear—"If you can't do it right, don't do it at all."

And now I was hearing that I had failed. You have to understand that my family was *not* saying this (there were no pointing fingers, no accusatory remarks), my family was saying I had a disease. They were saying, "Mother, you're sick, we love you and we want to help you." But what I heard was that I had let them down.

My self-esteem was nonexistent. I did not understand how much love it took for them to risk this confrontation with me. For months, I had been withdrawing. As I got sicker, I gradually stopped going to lunch, I wouldn't see friends, I was putting everyone out of my life.

So far as my family was concerned, a crisis point had been reached a few months before, at Christmas. The children say it was the worst Christmas ever, but I was completely oblivious to their distress. I thought everyone was happy. We were up in Vail, where we'd always come for the holidays, there was a lot of good snow, we were together, and I had my pills.

I did notice that anyone who prepared a drink for me kept it very light, and I would say, "Oh, for heaven's sake, if you're going to make me a drink, make me a real drink, or else just give me plain tonic." But that was the extent of my awareness that I was being watched.

Our oldest son, Mike, reports that was the week the children went to Jerry. And since I was pretty much *hors de combat,* I'm going to depend on the fighters who were *not* disabled to fill in what happened.

Mike Ford: "We said something's wrong here, but we were in the dark about drug dependency and alcoholism. We didn't know what we were up against, we just knew Mother was manifesting a lot of unhealthy signs, being incoherent, kind of shuffling around, not eating right. And the slurred speech, the not getting dressed until late in the day, had become a lifestyle. You could tell she was a sick woman, but none of us—not even Dad—knew what to do. We all just kind of said, 'We'll try to spend more time with her, be more in touch with her.' And Dad said he wouldn't travel as much."

Susan Ford Vance: "Even earlier, in the desert, I had talked to Dad. He was as frustrated as I was. It was one of those 'Well, sweetheart, you find the solution and I'm with you,' but he didn't know what to do either. It was like there was this disease, and who do you talk to about it?"

Jerry Ford: "Susan had been talking to me about 'Mother's problem,' but I guess she was somewhat intimidated by me because she never really came out and said, 'Dad, you've got to do something.' "

Finally, it was Susan herself who did something. Through the grace of God, I guess, she got involved with helping Joe Cruse— Dr. Joseph Cruse—up at Turnoff, which is a rehabilitation center for chemically dependent kids. Dr. Cruse was our gynecologist, and a recovering alcoholic, and he had hired Susan to take pictures of Turnoff so he could raise some money for it. On their way up there, they discussed my case.

Susan Ford Vance: "I said, 'Dr. Cruse, I've got this friend, and she's got a problem,' and he said, 'Susan, your friend is your mother, isn't she?' And I said yeah.

"He said he could help me put an intervention team together, and I said, 'Well, let me go back to my dad, because I couldn't okay anything without him.' I wasn't married yet, Chuck and I weren't even engaged then.

"So I went back and talked to Dad, and he said, 'That sounds great,' and then he took off on a trip. So I called Clara back in Washington. Clara Powell had worked for our family all the time we kids were growing up, she had been our second mother. And I said, 'Clara, you've got to come out here. Mother is taking pills, and I can't stand it anymore. The boys keep telephoning and

9

asking how she is, and I don't know what to tell them. I don't even want to see her every day because it frustrates me.'

"I was upset when I did see my mother, and my mother was upset when I didn't see her. I wasn't living with my parents, I had my own place, and when I'd go over to my dad's office, Mother would hear I had been there, right next door, and hadn't stopped by the house, and she'd get hurt.

"Clara promised she would come out—ostensibly to help Mother get everything in the new house unpacked and settled— and I talked to Dr. Cruse again, and he said, again, 'We can do it if your father is willing.' "

Dr. Joseph Cruse: "Almost as soon as we got in the car to drive to Turnoff, Susan grabbed my arm and said, 'Can you help my mother?' Just blurted it out.

"I said yes, and about a week later, I got a call from Bob Barrett, who had been President Ford's Army aide in the White House, and who, as a civilian, still worked with the family. He asked who I was and why I was involving myself in the Fords' personal affairs. He really raked me over the coals, and I thought, who needs this? But I explained what Susan and I had been talking about, and the next night, Barrett had me come over and explain to the President what an intervention was."

Before Jerry could make up his mind one way or another about the wisdom of a full-scale intervention, Susan and Joe Cruse attempted a mini-intervention of their own.

I was in the study when they arrived, and they brought with them Clara and Caroline Coventry, who was my secretary. And Joe started sharing with me the history of his drinking problems, and I thought, what a bunch of pips they are to have dreamt this up. It seemed so underhanded for Susan and Clara and Caroline to gang up on me, and bring in a stranger. Of course, I knew Joe Cruse as a gynecologist, but I already had an internist I saw every Tuesday at twelve noon, and nobody had sent for *him.* Now suddenly this Dr. Cruse comes out of the woodwork, and the only thing in my mind was, let me get rid of him.

Joe Cruse: "I had put on a tie, which you don't normally do in the desert, in order to go and see Mrs. Ford. I went over and spent an hour and a half telling her my story, and just as I was getting to the point I thought might sell her, she fell asleep. I woke her up and told her the rest of it, and I said I thought she too had a chemical dependency problem. She was very gracious, and thanked me for my interest.

"Then Susan and Caroline and I went out on the driveway, and I said to Susan, 'You better go back in there and hug your mother, I just threw a big bunch of stuff at her.' So Susan went tearing in, and came tearing out again, and she said, 'She's hugging Clara, she doesn't want to hug me, and she wants you off this property and don't you ever come back!' "

Susan's recollection diverges from Joe's in at least one respect. It doesn't include an iota of graciousness on my part. According to her, our meeting was a disaster.

Susan Ford Vance: "We told Mother she had to stop, and she said, 'Well, I am stopping, I've cut out this pill, I've cut out that pill,' and she got so mad at us, and she was already so high anyway —we didn't catch her early enough in the morning—that she looked at me and Caroline and Dr. Cruse and she said, 'You are all a bunch of monsters. Get out of here and never come back.'

"She kicked us out.

"I was devastated. Here Dr. Cruse had promised me that we were going to help my mother, and all we'd done was fall flat on our faces, and my mother had kicked me out of her house.

"I went home and later that night I called Clara, because at that point, Clara was the only person Mother would talk to. And boy, was I glad she was there. She said, 'Don't worry, Mother's fine. I've got her settled down.' "

They had me settled down and settled up and settled. Two days later, they did the intervention. The real thing. Thursday to Saturday was all it took for them to put it together.

11

Bob Barrett: "Everybody had been trying to figure out the best time to have the intervention, but they were also sort of avoiding it. We were in Rochester, where President Ford had been speaking, when we got the call. Mrs. Ford had to go into treatment right away. It was very late Friday, but the President phoned Mike and Gayle and asked them to fly to Palm Springs right away. President Ford was supposed to speak in Virginia the next day, and in New York City the day after that, but he got Henry Kissinger to agree to fill in these dates, and then we flew home in a private jet, arriving in the early morning. The Ford kids were already there, and at 7:30 A.M. in the President's office, we were taught how to conduct an intervention."

Jerry Ford: "It all came to a head after Susan and Cruse had gone to Betty and she'd thrown them out. It was obvious something had to be done. I recognized the intervention was a gamble, but at that point, I felt the risk was worth taking."

Bill Bloomer: "My wife and I were out in Palm Springs when they did the intervention on my sister Betty. And Susan got hold of me and said, 'I've gone through this preparation, and we're going to confront Mother, and she is going to immediately call you for help. And I just hope you won't give her any.' And I said, 'Oh, no, I agree with you a hundred percent. And I think I should talk to Jerry, because he is so in love with Betty and so protective and I've got to tell him he's going to have to be tough.' And I did tell him that, and he said he knew. He said he realized it was going to be probably the hardest thing he ever did."

Dr. Joseph Pursch: "It was on a Thursday that Joe Cruse called me at the naval hospital and said Mrs. Ford needed to have an intervention. He told me how much medication she was on, and I knew she would need to be detoxed slowly, but I thought it could be done perfectly safely in her house. Because Dr. Cruse's office was close by—he was right in Palm Springs—and he'd explained that the Fords lived only minutes from the emergency room at Eisenhower Hospital if anything should go wrong.

12

"I said I would come to Palm Springs the next day, Friday, and I would bring my nurse, Pat Benedict, with me. There were several reasons for this. Pat was under my command, and I could have the naval hospital give her a set of orders, no questions asked, so this would not become a public matter, and Pat could live at the Ford residence.

"Also, Pat was a fully trained nurse, and a recovering alcoholic. She could help Mrs. Ford to understand the disease concept."

Pat Benedict: "Dr. Pursch called me and asked me to come by his house. It was a Thursday night. When I got there, he took me into the living room, and asked me what I knew about Betty Ford. I said I didn't know anything about Betty Ford, and he looked at me like I was weird. He said he had been talking to Dr. Cruse and we were going to do an intervention, and we would take it a step at a time.

"I went on emergency leave—Pursch told people at the hospital that my mother had had a heart attack, so for days my mother was getting get-well cards, and wondering where I was—and on Friday, we drove to Palm Springs, and went directly to Joe Cruse's office. Cruse and Susan and Clara were there, and Clara said, 'Looks like we have a team.' I spent that night at Dr. Cruse's house, and it was arranged that we would all meet early the next morning in President Ford's office."

Joe Pursch: "Because we met with Clara and Susan that Friday afternoon, I had a chance to fill them in a little before the rest of the family arrived. 'What we want to do tomorrow,' I said, 'is have this lady in a position where she won't run out. So there must not be any heated discussions or arguments. We want to present to her, lovingly but firmly, brief facts about two things—how her illness is affecting and destroying her, and how her illness is affecting and destroying you.

" 'And how, as her daughter and her friend, you can no longer stand by and watch.' Then I asked what they could fill me in on, and Susan said, 'Well, she's on medication, and she's taking

13

it for pain. I know that, but it makes me angry and it makes me worried, and I'm afraid she'll die.' And I said, 'This is what you need to tell her.' "

Susan Ford Vance: "When I met Pat Benedict, it was like somebody had just taken a hundred-pound weight off my head. Because she understood what I was going through. I mean, I'd tell her stories and she'd heard them all before, and she convinced me that my mother was not the strangest person I had met in my entire life.

"And Clara's being there was good too. I think it was Clara who finally called my brother Jack and convinced him to take part in the intervention. He was the one most against it, but Clara said, 'We've got to do this for Mother. If we lose, we lose, but we will have given it our best shot.' So finally, Jack came around."

Jack Ford: "After you've buried somebody three times over, you're probably a little reluctant to start shoveling dirt again. I had given up hope that the problem would ever be corrected, and I didn't want to hurt her gratuitously, I guess."

Mike Ford: "Susan was the one who said we just could not go on like this, she was the one who told Dad, get your rear end home, Mother is in a bad way. When Dad called Gayle and me, he said, 'We want to do this right away. Can you fly out?'

"He said we all needed to be there to make a unified presentation, that the intervention would be an act of love to help Mother and the family.

"I was scared of Mother's reaction. I knew we had to face up to the problem, but I was deeply unsure about what the results of this step would be.

"Then, I think, with the advice of Dr. Pursch and Dr. Cruse —we needed some coaching—we began to understand the nature of chemical dependence, and how it had taken over her life, and at that point, I was really prepared to march in there and lay it on her."

14

Steve Ford: "I hadn't been around that much. I'd come visit, but Susan lived in Palm Springs, and that's why she stirred the pot up. She got burned the worst. The rest of us were off in our own areas, and didn't have to be personally involved. It's hard to live with anyone who has a drug or alcohol problem. They don't think rationally all the time, they don't act rationally, they don't understand.

"We as a family were frustrated with it, but we never made the initial push to do something about it. We kept avoiding it. We had never given Mom a chance to have our support in solving her problem.

"If she hadn't wanted to correct it, well then, we would have had to say, 'Mother, we love you, we're there for you, but we can't do this for the rest of our lives,' and we would have had to move on. But we'd never even given her the chance, we'd never tried it. I think there was some guilt about that.

"I was not educated in the treatment of alcoholics or drug abuse. I wasn't sure what was going to happen. When I drove down to the desert that Saturday morning, I wasn't sure what the whole thing was about. It wasn't until we got together over in Dad's office with the doctors and my brothers and sister that I found out what we were going to do."

Pat Benedict: "They had just moved from a rented house in the desert, everything was still in boxes in the new house and the office. When President Ford came into the office, the kids were already there. The President looked very stern, very much in control.

"I don't remember whether it was Pursch or Cruse who explained about telling their mother their feelings, but it seems to me we were not there very long.

"It was brought out that if Mrs. Ford understood and agreed to treatment, I would stay with her until her treatment was decided on, and when Dr. Pursch said, 'Doesn't anybody have anything to say?' I said, 'I have one thing.' And I said to President Ford, 'I will do all I can to help your wife,' and he just looked at me and said thank you."

15

Joe Pursch: "During the pre-intervention, Jack Ford was the one who needed reassurance that this was necessary. He said to me, 'You know, you haven't met this patient,' and that was true. But I told him I had seen the list of medications that had been dispensed to her."

Bob Barrett: "Before they left the office, Pursch had given them all instructions, and they got a little nitpicky like people do. Everybody started taking shots at one another, and I have a big mouth, so I got into it. I said, 'I just don't think you should all be after one another, assessing blame, I just don't see that working.' I talked to Pursch later and he said, 'Those people are scared. They've never done anything like this before. The idea is to get them comfortable enough so someone does some risk taking, gets a little more eloquent than he normally is, makes a good point in a kind manner.' "

Joe Cruse: "It took us only about fifteen minutes down in the President's office to train the family. They were so ready. Pursch and I handed them pieces of paper and said, 'Now you have to write down some event and how you felt about it, and then another event and how you felt about it.' And they were all writing, and then one of them would read aloud what he had written—his mother had fallen asleep in front of his friends, and he'd had to take her upstairs, something like that—and one of the others would say, 'Dad, do you hear that? Do you hear that?' And the President just listened, really listened to all of it."

Jerry Ford: "The doctors literally gave us a set of instructions, guidelines we had to follow to make the intervention successful. And they warned the kids in advance, 'Now your mother's going to get mad, your mother's going to cry, she's going to resent it, she may even get up and walk out, but you have to be firm, you have to be straightforward, and you can't let her intimidate you because that's what she's been doing, she has browbeaten all of you.'

"And that was true. I had turned into an enabler myself. I

16

was making it possible for Betty to continue to drink and take pills. I would make all kinds of alibis about why we were late getting someplace, or why Betty didn't show up at all. And it was getting worse, not better. My pleading with her was not helping. In fact, it was exacerbating the situation, because she would resent it as though nothing was wrong, and I was being a nitpicker.

"So this intervention was a last chance. I knew I would hate the things I had to say, but I was relieved too. I was convinced this was the only way the situation could be turned around. It was a dead-end street, the way we were going."

Joe Pursch: "After the pre-intervention session, I gave the family a coffee break, to get their nerves settled. I told them Joe Cruse and Pat and I would meet them over at the house in ten minutes, and we would hold the intervention.

"Sometimes, you have to hold several of these pre-intervention sessions. If the family you're working with is very disjointed, if there are several people there who have drinking problems, if the sick person's husband or wife already has some other wife or husband in mind. Then you hold these meetings over a course of a couple of weeks, and you make your decisions—we can't use the maid, we can't use the sister, the husband is iffy. But the Fords were really right there. They had been dispersed all over, but they came together like a magnet.

"When the President walked into his office so early that morning, he was tired. He said, 'This is not going to be pleasant, is it?' And I said, 'No, it's never pleasant, but it's the only thing to do. When it works, it works beautifully and is life-saving.'

"At the end of our little training session, he spoke again. 'Are you sure this needs to be done? And that she can be helped?' I said, 'I'm positive about the first, and I'm highly optimistic about the second.'

" 'In that case,' he said, 'we'll go.' And he put down his pipe, and stood up."

When the whole family trooped into the house, I had no clue what was coming. I thought Mike and Gayle had flown out to visit

17

because I hadn't been feeling well, and I was absolutely delighted. Until Jerry sat me down on that couch and said, "Mother, we've got something to talk to you about, and we want you to listen, because we love you."

I listened, but I didn't hear that they loved me. I heard that I had failed.

Steve Ford: "She never failed. I can understand how she could think that, when this thing happened, but she never failed as a mother. At the intervention, I only told one story, of a weekend when Dad was gone, and he didn't want Mom to be alone, so Melanie, the girl I was going with, and I drove to Palm Springs. And when we got there, I made dinner. I fixed vegetables, salad, the whole thing, and took it in to Mom, and she said, 'Oh, thank you, but I really don't feel like eating,' and I was hurt. I'd gone to the store, done the shopping, put the silverware on the proper sides of the plates, and she went and got another drink.

"When I told that at the intervention, she cried. You know, there were a lot of things coming out that had never been said before."

Jack Ford: "The only point I made at the intervention—it was a point I felt very strongly about—was that I hadn't liked to bring friends home. If somebody came by the house, particularly if we'd gone out to the movies first, something like that, I was always kind of peeking around the corner into the family room to see what kind of shape Mother was in."

Mike Ford: "I told Mother that, being the oldest, I thought I probably saw more clearly the strain on her of having been a wife in Washington, and the mother of four children, and all the pressures and demands that had created her environment. But I said she had got to the point now where her lifestyle was very destructive, she was hurting her relationships with her husband, her family and her friends, and that those relationships were too valuable to lose, and that her life was too valuable to let go.

"Then Gayle said something that hit really hard. We had

18

been married about four years, and Gayle's comment to Mother was that we wanted to start a family, and we wanted our children to know their grandmother, and not only know her but know her as a healthy, loving person. At that point, she had no grandchildren, and the prospect of not living to see her grandchildren, or living in such a miserable state that the grandchildren would be afraid of her—that really knocked her flat."

Bob Barrett: "President and Mrs. Ford were sitting in front of the window, their backs to the golf course. They were the only ones on the sofa. Then all around them in a circle were Mike and Gayle, Jack and Steve and Susan and Clara and the doctors and the nurse.

"Mrs. Ford looked small, almost like a doll, lost in the cushions, and as her husband made his opening remarks, you could see the confusion in her face. He was saying she was chemically dependent, 'and the doctors want to talk to you,' and then Dr. Pursch said, 'Mrs. Ford, you don't have to be alarmed, all these people care for you.'

"Then Mike spoke. It had begun. The game was on, and you could see Mrs. Ford reeling. Here comes this avalanche of love, and yet with it a devastating appraisal of the person's shortcomings. I looked at Pursch because I thought, I'll bet that's what's supposed to happen. And the President moved even closer to Mrs. Ford, and she got even smaller.

"Jack talked, Steve talked, and then it came to Susan. She was the youngest, she was the girl, she was responsible for bringing this whole thing together, she thought she was going to have everything to say, and then she totally broke down. Up till then, everyone had been tender, but no one had broken down. Susan turned to Clara and put her head on her chest, and Clara just stroked her, and said, 'Now, now.' "

Susan Ford Vance: "Dad started by saying the reason we're here is we love you. Everybody kept saying the reason we're here is we love you. Pursch had told us if she got any feeling of animosity, forget it. And he'd also told us to write down the things we wanted to say so we wouldn't forget them. So I had written down the fact that she'd always been a dancer, and I had always admired her for being a dancer, but these days she was falling and clumsy, and she just wasn't the same person. And I had talked to her about things that were important to me, and she hadn't remembered them, and it had really hurt my feelings.

"I had never said any of this before, but it had been building up in me for a long time. I guess I had been aware that Mother took pills when we were in the White House, but I hadn't thought twice about it until much later. When I dropped out of college and came home in the spring of 1977, I began to notice that since she'd moved to the desert, she had no close friends anymore. And I thought, poor Mother, isn't she lonely here by herself?

"Then I really started to see it. Once she fell in the middle of the night and cracked her ribs and chipped her tooth.

"I had started dating Chuck—he was at that time one of my parents' Secret Service agents—and he was with her on different assignments, protecting her, and he would come to me later and say, 'Susan, you've got to do something about your mother, she's slowly destroying herself.' I was getting pressure from him because his father was an alcoholic who eventually committed suicide. It caused terrible arguments between us, and now I look at him and think, thank you for keeping after me about it.

"I remember going to Las Vegas with Mother to see Tony Orlando in a show. And Chuck and I had to just about carry her upstairs to her room. Everybody covered for her, we were perfect at covering for her, and all the while we were thinking, what are we going to do?

"At the intervention, it took me a long time to get any words out, not just because I was crying, but because Mother was crying so hard, and that bothered me, but at the same time, it was almost healing for me, it was like peeling away all the layers, for once it was out in the open."

Pat Benedict: "When Susan talked, she crumpled. I scooted my chair over beside her—I had met her the day before, which made a difference—and she took my hand and squeezed it so tight she damn near broke it."

Joe Cruse: "When we all went into the house, Betty was surprised to see Mike and Gayle, and she hugged them, and then she realized there were these strangers along with her family. And the President sat holding her, and I was wondering, 'Who's going to start?' and Pursch was wondering, 'Who's going to start?' and Pat Benedict was wondering, 'Who's going to start?' and the President started. Betty already knew me but the President introduced her to Joe Pursch and Pat Benedict. He told Betty the family loved her and was worried about her, 'and we have people here who are going to help us, and we want you to just sit and listen.' Then he flipped around and pointed his finger and said, 'Mike, you start.'

"The President took over and ran the intervention. I said zero, Pat said zero, Pursch said zero. And that's a miracle."

The whole thing was a miracle. It's a miracle I didn't just not wake up some morning from all the drugs I was taking, and it's a miracle my family didn't just let me slip away.

I think the intervention worked because we are so close. Even when the kids were small, and Jerry and I wanted to buy a place in Vail, we asked their opinions. We wanted to be sure Vail was where they'd enjoy spending every summer, every Christmas vacation.

Any major decision has always involved all of us, and my recovery involved all of us, because my disease involved all of us.

But I also think if any one of the kids—or Jerry—had tried to intervene, I could have turned it around. I could have said, "I'm glad you told me, I'll take care of it, don't worry." And gone on getting sicker and sicker because I'd have been adding guilt, and compounding the problem.

But they all came together, and they came before I had completely destroyed myself.

Which does not mean I enjoyed the intervention.

When Pursch said, "Well, I guess you don't have any brain

damage," I was flabbergasted. Brain damage? My God, brain damage. It was something I'd never thought of.

When Steve did that bit about cooking for me—"and you had one drink, two drinks, and wouldn't come to dinner"—I thought, that kid has a lot of nerve. I was *used* to having two drinks before dinner.

When Susan came off as the perfect daughter, I felt some resentment about that too. As I look back, I realize I had no comprehension of my disease. My denial was at its peak, and denial is a cornerstone of alcoholism.

And I didn't enjoy Jerry's reference to the night I fell and cracked my ribs either. One of my points of pride was that I *didn't* ever fall down. Could I have been having blackouts from time to time? Not remembering what had really happened?

Jerry said how slow I was, how tardy. "You were in second gear," he said. And he said it had become "increasingly difficult to lead a normal life."

I believe my husband had got to the point where he thought he simply had a wife who was no longer a strong woman (after all, she was seeing a doctor every week, and the doctor wasn't telling her not to come back), and having had all those babies had worn her out, and she'd had that bad experience with the pinched nerve in her neck, and she'd been in and out of hospitals; she was just one of those unfortunate women who were going to fade away, and there was nothing he could do about it.

It was easier for him to travel. He said it used to upset him to watch me get up in the morning and take that handful of pills, and then take another handful at night, on top of a couple of drinks, before we went to bed.

A lot of the time, he just turned away, pretending not to see, his denial of my condition as firmly in place as my own. While we were still renting, while our house was being built at Thunderbird, he would try to speak optimistically to the kids. "Well," he would say, "she'll be better when we get down in the house on the golf course, because she'll have the dogs, and she can walk them on the golf course, and that will be good for her, and keep her occupied; she'll have something to do."

As for the boys, when Susan first went to Joe Cruse, I'm not sure her brothers didn't resent her interference, though that interference saved my life. Or maybe what saved my life was that the intervention made me see how much they all cared about me.

When you're suffering from alcoholism, or any other drug dependency, your self-esteem gets so low you're sure nobody would want to bother with you. I think intervention works because suddenly you realize somebody *is* willing to bother, somebody cares.

Not that an intervention could work if the patient were dead set against it. The family can't say, okay, we're going to physically put you in this hospital and lock all the doors and windows and you'll stay there till you're better. Something in me had to respond, to think maybe there is something wrong, maybe I do take the wrong pills, or too many of them, maybe I am getting dependent on them.

At the end of the intervention, Dr. Pursch asked me if I was willing to go into treatment, and I said yes, but Bob Barrett claims I didn't sound wholehearted. He says I was using my "professional political smile," and uttering hollow-sounding platitudes about how I wanted to be well.

Dr. Pursch said, "That's fine, Mrs. Ford," and then Pat Benedict crossed the room to me, and I wondered what she wanted. I'd had to agree to let this woman stay with us.

Pat Benedict: "It was my understanding that number one, we've got to get her detoxed, and number two, we've got to get her into treatment. I didn't know if she would be going to Hazelden, or the naval hospital, or China.

"I knelt in front of her, and I didn't say a word about alcohol, only about drugs. I said, 'Betty, I have had a problem too—I took a lot of amphetamines in Vietnam, and some Valium to level the nerves—and I will help you.' She looked at me like, I don't really give a damn, and I said, 'Betty, I also have had a breast removed,' and she reached out and patted me on the cheek. That got her attention."

Before they went to lunch—they left me alone with my family for a while—the doctors told me they'd be coming back with some friends, and for me to get dressed. Naturally, I wasn't dressed, I was in a robe. And they said they would be collecting all my medications and prescriptions and taking them away.

I got dressed, and put myself together to prove how really well I was. I also swallowed a bunch of pills. I'd show them. They were going to confiscate my supply? I'd just gulp down the four or five pills I normally took at noon; I might need them before this day was over.

In the afternoon, some people came and showed us how support group meetings work. They all told their stories. About their alcoholism and their recovery and how changed their lives were now.

Still sedated to the teeth, I was perfectly amenable. I thought, isn't this nice? And I remember one of the women had brought me a box of Kleenex tied up with colored yarn, and she said, "Here, you'll need this when you go to treatment," and I thought, I'm not going to cry anymore, I'm cried out, I'm numb.

After this group meeting, Dr. Pursch gave us a lecture. Using a blackboard, he listed every drug I was on, how many milligrams a day of each, and when he added them all up, the amount was staggering. He said over the years I had developed an amazing tolerance for this medication.

When they confront you with that kind of evidence on a blackboard, you have to be a real dummy not to realize you're in trouble.

Jerry Ford: "My apprehension about the amount of medication had been growing. I never counted the pills, but I knew she took a lot; I saw the bills from the pharmacy. I was more concerned with the drugs than with the alcohol, because the amounts she was drinking didn't seem abnormally high. It was a couple of vodkas before dinner, and after dinner she would want a couple of bourbons. But I did not know how the combination of alcohol and pills multiplied the impact until Pursch showed us that chart. It was the first concrete evidence I'd seen."

Pursch said that once I was detoxed, there were several alternatives for me to consider, so far as treatment was concerned. I could go to meetings of Alcoholics Anonymous, and learn to live a sober, drug-free life, but that would take longer than if I went into a concentrated treatment program. Hazelden, outside of Minneapolis, was suggested, and so was Dr. Pursch's rehab unit at the naval hospital in Long Beach.

I chose Long Beach because I wanted to stay in California. Steve was in Laguna, Jack in San Diego and Susan in Palm Springs, and I didn't want to be far away from them.

Susan Ford Vance: "So then the process began of going through the whole house cleaning out the drugs. Dr. Cruse and Caroline Coventry and I took everything and anything we could get our hands on, even over-the-counter stuff. There were bottles and bottles and bottles. We threw them into a box, and Cruse took the box away.

"Everything went like clockwork. Mother didn't like Pat at first, but she cooperated. A movie projector arrived, and they started bringing in educational films about alcohol and drug dependency for all of us to watch so we could begin to figure out what was going on.

"Clara, I remember, made pot roast that night, and we all had dinner together. It was like the family was a family once again. It was like everything had been torn down, and there was nothing to hide anymore."

Pat Benedict: "Jack and Steve put up a rollaway bed for me in the study close to the Fords' bedroom. When Pursch went back to Long Beach, he didn't even say goodbye to me, he just left me down there. Didn't say lots of luck or anything. He was my boss, and he just left. He had Cruse and me go to Eisenhower and get the medicine to detoxify Betty at home. I've said to Pursch since, we were either very brilliant, or very lucky. She could have died."

25

Steve Ford: "Mom was a very scared woman, left naked to say she was addicted. And in fact, forced to say it, we kind of didn't give her a choice. When I look back, I see this vision of her shaking. Someone came in and took all the pills from her bathroom and dressing room, all the things she could hide behind. When she first started down the road to recovery, I don't think she had any idea where it was going."

I didn't, oh, I didn't.

That week of detoxification, I shook so much I didn't need an electric toothbrush. And in bed at night, my legs kept moving, I couldn't lie still. I kept saying the Serenity Prayer—"God grant me the serenity to accept the things I cannot change . . ." I did it by rote, as I struggled through the chemical withdrawal that brought on the agitation. Repeating it over and over gave me a sense of the now, it seemed to calm me.

It took a lot of prayer, a lot of exercise, a lot of soaks in the Jacuzzi, to get me ready for sleep. Sometimes I couldn't sleep anyway. I'd be up before anyone else in the morning, and I'd put the coffee on. I'd wander through the house, I'd stretch out on the floor, I'd watch the hummingbirds wake up outside the windows. And what I found out is, you don't die from lack of sleep, you'll sleep when your body is ready. My body wasn't ready.

There are still nights when I wish I had a sleeping pill, but sleeping pills are from another life, and I've learned to do without that crutch. I get up, have a glass of milk and a graham cracker, read a while. It would be easier if my husband weren't so sane and put together. He makes me furious because when I'm lying there worrying about some problem, he will say, "You can't do anything about it tonight, you may as well go to sleep so you'll be rested, and can tackle it tomorrow." He's wonderful, and I want to smack him.

I think now it was rather chancy for them to try to detox me at home the way they did. I think I should have been in a hospital, and Pat agrees with me.

26

Pat Benedict: "I don't know why Pursch and Cruse didn't take her over to Eisenhower. I wouldn't be surprised if she still had some anger over that. I know I was very scared, I thought, what am I doing here? I'm not even a Republican! Sick as she was, they felt this was what she needed, they don't think they abandoned her, they think they did what was best for her.

"The very first day after the intervention, she was really sick. She kept throwing up."

Susan Ford Vance: "I came by, and Dad was there, and I said, 'How's Mom, can I see her?' And he said, 'Oh, she's really sick to her stomach, I wouldn't go in and bother her.' And I thought, if I'd known what she was going to have to go through, I'm not sure I would have voted for it."

Pat Benedict: "President Ford was scared too. He wanted to know why Betty kept throwing up. I said, 'Mr. President, this is the worst day she'll ever have. I will have her up and bathed and walking tomorrow.'

"Next day she and I did go for a walk on the golf course—we went past the President's office, and she waved to him. She was wearing a blue skirt, and she had a bandana around her head, and I carried Valium and a syringe and a tourniquet in my pocket, in case of an emergency. And as we continued along the path, all of a sudden she reached over and put her arm around me. And I thought, we're going to be okay.

"She wanted to get well, and that's half the battle."

The week passed. Pat was on the phone to Dr. Cruse and Dr. Pursch about my blood pressure, about my shots, about my dry heaves, the whole business. I took my last Librium—you're weaned away from your pills by slow degrees—at midnight, Friday, April 7. Steve was there, and he and Pat and I celebrated in the kitchen with glasses of cranapple juice.

Saturday was my sixtieth birthday, and I was supposed to go next door to the Firestones' for dinner. I didn't want to do it. I knew there would be a cocktail hour, and I didn't want to face that, and I was having terrible neck pains, and of course I had no pain medication.

Pat Benedict: "The pinched nerve was hurting her, and they had this dinner planned, just Leonard and Nicky Firestone and Dolores Hope and the President and Betty. And Betty just said she wasn't going to go. And Clara and Caroline and I looked at each other, and then I called Dr. Pursch and said, 'She doesn't want to go.' He said, 'I want her up and dressed and at that party.'

"So we got her up and dressed, and once she and the President crossed the lawn to the Firestone house, Clara and Susan and I went into town. It was the first time I'd been out since I came down there. Clara bought our dinner, but I was worried the whole time. I thought, God, I know she isn't going to stay at that party. Well, she did stay. All evening. And when she came home, she said, 'It was really a nice evening,' and I thought, I could just kick your tail."

Nicky Firestone: "She called and said she didn't think she could make it to our house for her birthday dinner. I said, 'Betty, you're among friends. If you swing from the chandelier, nobody's going to think anything of it. Do what you can. We very much want you to come. If you don't feel up to the whole evening, fine, do any part of it.'

"She came, and when dinner was announced, she stepped right up to the table, and she and Jerry never went home till eleven o'clock."

It happened just that way. I not only stayed through the cocktail hour, I stayed through dinner, and I marveled that I was able to eat some soup without shaking and slopping it all over the table.

On Sunday, Pat packed my bag for Long Beach. I would be going there the next morning.

I'd had my last drink on March 31, the night before the intervention.

It was more than forty years since I'd had my first.

3

They are not long, the days of wine and roses.
                                    Ernest Dowson

Listen, they're long enough.

It takes a long time for alcohol and/or pills to kill you. Somebody once told Robert Benchley the liquor he was drinking was slow poison, and Benchley shrugged. "So who's in a hurry?" he said.

It took a long time for me to get where I'd got, trying to decide what kind of clothes to take so I could go hang out with a bunch of sailors. I even insisted on shopping for new slacks so I could go looking my very best.

I don't intend to offer here an unabridged chronicle of my using and my drinking. Still, it might be edifying to take a short look back down the road that brought me, finally, to the naval hospital.

For openers, a lot of the journey seemed enjoyable.

I think of the first beer I ever had. It was at Bennington College, where I went to study dance the summer I was eighteen. My roommate and I, convinced we were drunk, ran around the campus acting crazy in the moonlight. Because we were happy, and thought we were such big stuff.

I think of my first trip to Europe, in 1956, and a train from Italy to Austria, and Jerry and me drinking our whiskey out of paper cups. We iced it with fresh snow we scooped up off the windowsill of our compartment, and laughed ourselves to sleep.

I think of a New Year's Eve in Vail. Watergate and my mastectomy were behind us, we were surrounded by people we loved, and we toasted in 1975, and drank enough to take care of several other years while we were at it.

I think of vacations, christenings, rituals, festivals, of lunch drinks and dressing drinks while we were preparing to go out, and nightcaps before bed. I think of that first sip of an icy martini. I think of Jerry and me sharing wine out of a German betrothal cup at our wedding rehearsal dinner.

Drinking was a way we relaxed, a way we celebrated, and it was good until it went bad. If you're not alcoholic, it doesn't have to go bad, but I'm alcoholic. I just didn't know it for thirty years.

I first tasted liquor when I was twelve or thirteen in the pantry of a girlfriend's house in Grand Rapids. Three or four of us kids tried it, said, "Oh, how awful," and went our ways.

In fact, as a teenager, I was a bit of a Carrie Nation. One time Bill Warren, the boy I later married, slipped away from a dance to go have a nip in the parking lot, and when he came back, I slapped his face and told him not to call me anymore.

At nineteen, I had my first unpleasant encounter with alcohol. It was a cuba libre at a hotel in Grand Rapids. I had modeled in a fashion show, and some friends took me out afterward, and later, when I got home, my mother found me moaning in the bathroom and said, "What in the world is the matter?" and I said, "Oh, I just feel awful, I had a rum and Coke, it's called a cuba libre," and she said, "Thank goodness that's all that's wrong."

I was cured of cuba libres, but if my illness was a warning, I didn't recognize it as such.

Act Two. When I was living in New York and studying with Martha Graham, my roommate and I went to a college bash in New Haven. The boys served us something called purple passion, which was probably grape juice and grain alcohol. I had a kind of blackout. There were a few minutes when everything was sort of numb and vague. Again, I didn't take it as a warning.

Back home in Grand Rapids, I went to a Christmas party at

five o'clock one afternoon, and the hosts served planter's punch. It had oranges floating around in it, it tasted like fruit juice, and it made a lot of the girls sick. It didn't make me sick, but I did get sort of tight.

I had to teach a class in ballroom dancing at the high school later that night, and my date took me home to his mother and father, who gave me black coffee. I thought how worldly they were, and was reasonably pleased with myself because I was still on my feet, when so many of my companions were out on theirs.

I disapproved of passing out; it was foreign to my nature to be out of control.

I drank on dates because I wanted to be part of the group. Then as now, young people responded to peer pressure. I can remember a beach party where we had kegs of beer, and we played ball, and somebody passed around manhattans—they looked interesting, with cherries in them—and they made me so sick I never did drink another manhattan.

At home, my parents always served cocktails, come five o'clock. It was a habit, like brushing your teeth in the morning. Now, with the 20/20 vision of hindsight, I can see alcohol did not agree with me, but in those days, we didn't even know alcoholism was a disease, or that it might be inherited. We also didn't know that some alcoholics are born that way (in trouble from the very first time they drink) whereas others achieve alcoholism through years of working at it. We keep abusing the system until the system breaks down. We keep trying over and over to handle party drinking, like trying to handle the social mores of how to eat raw oysters on the half shell, or escargots. It all goes with the game, and it seems important to be good at it, to be accepted.

My father was alcoholic, though I never knew it until after he died, and so was my brother Bob. My brother Bill is rather baffled about how he escaped. "Drinking doesn't agree with me," he says mildly.

Wise brother Bill. I was less moderate than he. In my early twenties, I got myself engaged to one of his lawyer friends, but the romance didn't last long. I liked boys, I liked parties, I liked to stay up late and flirt, and the lawyer disapproved of all these enthusiasms. "He was a very sober fellow," I wrote in my first book. Sober didn't appeal to me, I thought it was synonymous with stuffy. I played with a wild bunch, or as wild as it got in Grand Rapids in the early forties.

So I married Bill Warren. Nothing stuffy about him. He had blond curly hair, he danced, he played tennis, and he was very popular.

Remember the old folk poem, "There is a tavern in the town, and there my true love sits him down, and drinks his wine with laughter and with glee, and never, never thinks of me"?

That was the story of my life with Bill Warren.

Still, when we went out together on Saturday nights, I drank right along with him and if, at the end of the evening, somebody suggested one for the road, I didn't say no. I didn't feel I *had* to have a drink, but I very seldom turned one down.

Eventually, I divorced Bill Warren. For all my rebellion, my yearning to break loose—hadn't I gone to New York to be a great dancer?—I was my mother's child. Hadn't I come home again? If I was going to be married, I wanted domestic tranquillity and babies, or why bother?

The marriage had lasted five years. For a while afterward, I was prudish about men and about liquor. I even stopped keeping liquor in my apartment. My brother Bob, who was by then a recovering alcoholic, and very active in helping others, used to come by with people he was trying to sober up. He said he liked to bring them there because he knew there was no beer in my refrigerator.

I can remember those fellows going out into my little kitchen and searching the shelves, hoping they'd find something, anything, even a bottle of vanilla extract. But if you wanted to drink when you came to my place, you had to bring it with you.

As for Jerry Ford, the most eligible bachelor (football hero, lawyer, ardent skier) in Grand Rapids, when I met him he scarcely drank at all. It just wasn't high on his list of priorities. At thirty-four, after four years in the Navy, he was again living at home. I think he just found it convenient to let his mother do his laundry.

The fall we got married, he made his first run for Congress, and he won a seat in the House of Representatives, and we moved to Washington. In Washington, there is more alcohol consumed per capita than in any other city in the United States. A prodigious amount of entertaining is done, and as a congressman, you are invited to most of it. Lobbyists give parties, so do senators and cabinet members and ambassadors. There are cocktail parties, receptions, dinners, fund-raisers, sometimes three a night, every night.

I probably encouraged my husband to drink. He was such a reserved man it was difficult for him even to tell me he loved me —he had proposed by saying, "I'd like to marry you." I wanted him to loosen up, so when he got in from work, I'd encourage him to have a beer or a martini to relax him. This kind of social hour had never been part of his experience, although he enjoyed it. But he never drank alcoholically, to make things better.

In my own mind, my drinking was simply convivial, and conviviality was fun. I liked our dinner guests to get a little mellow before we sat down to the table because it made for more successful parties, or so I thought.

Most of the time that Jerry was in Congress we lived in a nice family neighborhood in Virginia. Practically everybody belonged to the same Episcopal church, our kids were into everything— Scouts and Little League and Sunday school. And most of their activities seemed to take place at our house. I was in the PTA. I was a den mother. I spent days in the car ferrying children to the orthodontist and the eye doctor. Very middle American ordinary. From the outside, our life looked like a Norman Rockwell illustration.

The only thing wrong with the picture is that somewhere along the line, alcohol became too important in my life.

I just don't remember when I went from being a social drinker to being preoccupied with drinking, but I'm sure it was pretty gradual. If you go to enough cocktail parties, you start anticipating cocktail parties, and then when you aren't going to a cocktail party, you want the same kind of lift at home.

Virginia was a local option state, so in a restricted county, you had to buy liquor in state stores, and if you were entertaining at the country club, you took liquor with you, or kept it in a locker there. When Jerry and I went with friends to a resort for a weekend, we all packed bottles. I told myself Jerry liked to have a drink before dinner. It was the "in" way to travel, a perfectly accepted way to behave. People gave each other nice leather carrying cases with room inside for a couple of bottles and some glasses.

When Jerry was away—and as he became more important in Congress, he was often away—I'd have my five o'clock drink at a neighbor's house. Or even by myself, while talking on the phone with a neighbor. I'd have another while I was fixing dinner and then, after the kids were in bed, I'd build myself a nightcap and unwind by watching television.

There were danger signs, but I buried them in my subconscious and only dredged them up years later. Sure, I didn't drink in the morning, but as I got more honest with myself, I was able to remember occasions when I had put a tablespoon of vodka into my hot tea, and it gave me a warm, mellow feeling.

Did I know instinctively that this would help relieve my emptiness, just as it had soothed me when I was a teenager, and my mother had put me to bed with a cup of tea fortified with whiskey to help relieve a cold, or cramps?

Maybe it is that first drink that is the important one. Maybe it was as an adolescent that I first realized what pleasure and escape a drink could bring.

This is a point I want to make about alcoholism. It isn't the amount you drink, or the brand, it's how it affects you. It's the thing that happens to you psychologically, when you drink because you like the feeling it brings.

The person who is not alcoholic doesn't worry about whether they're going to serve drinks where he's going. I did worry about it. My husband would never have thought of drinking by himself. Obviously, as I look back, there were times when I not only thought about it, I did it.

The children were still young—Susan was five years old— when I developed a pinched nerve in my neck. The pinched nerve required many days of hospitalization in traction, physical therapy, hot packs, massage, acupuncture—and drugs. I remember telling one of the doctors at George Washington Hospital that I worried about going out. "I'm so afraid the pain will start."

"Don't *let* the pain start," he said. "Keep your medication with you, take it every four hours."

If I developed a tolerance for one drug, the doctors gave me another. I hated feeling crippled, I hated my body's rebellion, I hated that I was hunched over and had to go to bed at night in traction, so I took more pills. It doesn't matter whether it's pills or alcohol, it wipes out your pain.

Now I know that some of the pain I was trying to wipe out was emotional.

Jerry became Minority Leader of the House, and I was proud of him, he was doing a magnificent job. But I was beginning to feel sorry for myself. It was poor me, who do they think is making it possible for him to travel all over the United States giving all those speeches? He gets all the headlines and applause, but what about me?

On the one hand, I loved being "the wife of"; on the other hand, I was convinced that the more important Jerry became, the less important I became. And the more I allowed myself to be a doormat—I knew I was a doormat to the kids—the more self-pity overwhelmed me. Hadn't I once been somebody in this world?

Underneath, I guess I didn't really believe I had been somebody. My career with Martha Graham hadn't been a huge success—I had talent as a dancer, but I wasn't a great dancer—and my confidence had always been shaky. If I was pledged to a sorority in high school, I'd say, "Oh, that's because I've got two older brothers, and the girls like my brothers." Or, "That's because I can dance, and I'll be an asset when they do a show."

I couldn't accept that people liked me for myself. And I was self-conscious that I didn't have a college degree, though I figured if I acted smart, and looked smart, maybe strangers would think I was smart.

Uneducated. No Pavlova. And not half the woman my

mother had been. I was always measuring myself against impossible ideals—Martha, or my mother—and coming up short. That's a good recipe for alcoholism.

My mother was a wonderful woman, strong and kind and principled, and she never let me down. She was also a perfectionist, and tried to program us children for perfection. My mother never came to us with her problems, she just shouldered them. And she was my strongest role model, so when I couldn't shoulder my problems, I lost respect for myself. No matter how hard I tried, I couldn't measure up to my own expectations.

None of this did I know while I was living it. But because drinking relieved me of my feelings of inadequacy, I leaned on alcohol. There are a lot of women like me—I want to do a whole chapter on women alcoholics later in this book—who have done the church things and the book fairs and fixed meals and supervised homework, dedicated their days to their husbands and children, and have no selves, no sense of self.

I was a controlled drinker, no binges. When I went to parties, I was on my best behavior. I drank, but never too much. I always knew there would be more available at home. One of the reasons my drinking didn't have to escalate was that I had begun taking so much medication. If you get up in the morning and swallow a pill, you don't need a drink. The pain pill does the same thing a drink would do, it steadies your nerves. And God help us, it's a great deal more respectable.

In 1965, about a year after I began mixing pain medication with alcohol, I snapped. I packed my bag one afternoon, and decided to drive to the beach, take Susan with me, and let my whole ungrateful family worry about where I was and whether I was ever coming home. Poor Susan thought I was crazy, and was humiliated by the idea of having a madwoman for a mother. I don't know if there was any connection between my chemical dependency and my crack-up, and as crack-ups go, it wasn't major, but it sufficed. It got my family's attention.

I talked to a psychiatrist, and he said I'd been too busy trying to figure out everyone else's needs, that I'd had no time for Betty.

He said I had to start thinking I was valuable, not just as a wife and mother, but as myself. And to myself.

The psychiatrist didn't particularly encourage my drinking, but he didn't suggest I stop drinking either. If he had, I probably would have blanked that out. Anyway, he wasn't treating me for alcoholism, he was treating me for low self-esteem. (Many psychiatrists think if they get to the bottom of the emotional problem, there won't be a drinking problem. That's backwards. You have to get rid of the alcoholism before you can treat the emotional problem.) Besides, I saw no reason to discuss my drinking. I preferred to pretend everything would get better if I went back to dance class, or did some shopping, or took an afternoon off to write letters.

Jerry, who has always been supportive, blamed himself for a good deal of my misery. He once admitted to a reporter that, because of his schedule, I'd had to be both mother and father to the children. "In election years, I'd go to Michigan after Congress adjourned, be away for three weeks, come home for the weekend, go back to Michigan and my constituents for another three weeks. We always tried to take family vacations at Christmas and in the summer, and those were wonderful times. Still, much of the year I was gone."

I think, as I've already said, I was born alcoholic. The pressures of my life didn't suddenly *make* me an alcoholic, it just took a few years for the disease to develop and surface in force. At one point, I even stopped drinking for two years.

I was hospitalized for stomach trouble. The doctors checked stomach, gallbladder, kidneys, and they couldn't find anything wrong. Then they brought in a specialist who diagnosed my illness as pancreatitis. He said, "Young lady, if I were you, I would just stay on the other side of the room from the bar for a while."

I said fine. If he'd told me I should stay on the other side of the room from the bar for the rest of my life, I would have been deeply offended, and I would have questioned him. As it was, I took his advice.

Jerry asked some of my doctors whether drinking had been the cause of the pancreatitis. They said it was a possibility.

37

"Which shows you," he says, "what enablers the medical profession are. The overwhelming evidence is that drinking is a prime cause of pancreatitis, but they all sort of avoided that, and so I avoided it too."

I don't even remember how or where I started drinking again. It was probably a glass of wine at a dinner party. (Meri Bell and her husband, Del, once quit drinking for a year, and after the year was up, they bragged, "Aren't we great? Let's go celebrate." And they went right to the country club and got smashed.)

My brother Bill says he talked to Jerry about "Betty's problem" back before the White House. He remembers saying, "She takes one drink and she's affected by it. Either she's combining pills and booze, or it's something else." And Jerry reassured him. "If it gets serious, we'll do something."

Nobody wanted to admit it was serious. Friends who loved me denied the evidence of their own eyes. Sheika Gramshammer, who lives in Vail and has known us since the late sixties, says, "Okay, we saw sometimes she had one bourbon too many, but everybody does that once in a while. And the drugs she took were because of the pain. We all thought, poor darling, she can't get through an evening without pain pills. But we never thought of her as being alcoholic."

Pressed about whether or not she noticed my condition deteriorating over the years, Sheika still makes excuses. "When I first met Betty, she had such a vitality and personality, but I think it must have been a very hard life for her as a congressman's wife, and she had problems with her neck, and nobody ever gave a damn how is the congressman's wife doing, and she couldn't load her problems on him, and then all of a sudden he became President, and she was pushed into the public eye, and that is the cruelest eye anywhere, and it frightened her."

Truthfully, it was *better* in the White House. I flowered. Jerry was no longer away so much. And I was somebody, the First Lady. When I spoke, people listened. I could campaign for women's rights and against child abuse. I began to enjoy a reputation for candor, and was able to do some good; when I discussed my

38

mastectomy, women all over the country went in for breast examinations.

But the neck problem got worse, so my pills were always with me. Susan talks about "this little black case the doctor kept perpetually filled." Still, I did not drink alcoholically in the White House. There was too much at stake, too much responsibility, I was too heavily scheduled. What little drinking we did was confined to Camp David on a weekend, or drinks upstairs—there was a bar in the President's quarters—before we went to bed.

For anyone who thinks otherwise, let me tell you being an occupant of the White House is no breeze. You have no private life, the demands on your time are constant, you are under terrible pressure. We traveled fast. Often, abroad, exhaustion and pain would take over, and I would have to go to bed with hot packs and pills only to get up later to go to a state dinner. But those dinners and the honor of representing our country meant a lot to me.

It was when we left the White House and moved West that things got worse. Maybe they would have worsened anyway, I don't know. But I was bitter and depressed at Jerry's having lost the election after twenty-eight years of faithful service to the country. I thought the American people had made a big mistake.

In a sense, I was out of office too. As First Lady, there had been a lot of demands made of me. I had been equal to most of them, performed well and enjoyed my moment in the sun. People with low self-esteem crave reassurance from the outside world.

Now we had abandoned the place where we had spent our entire married life, the children were gone, even Susan had her own condominium, which we helped her buy in Palm Desert, and nobody needed me any longer. At least that's what I thought. And even though, in the early days of our marriage, I had sometimes resented all that needing, now I missed it.

After all the action I'd seen, it was an emotional shock to suddenly be home alone again at night, with my husband gone. Because Jerry's retirement was a fraud; he might as well have been campaigning, he was away teaching, lecturing, serving on the boards of ten or more business or charity organizations.

I'm not trying to make excuses, but I think when you are genetically predisposed to alcoholism, and you get caught up in just the right circumstances, your controls fall away, and the progression of your disease takes over. When the kids were small, and I was feeling put upon, the circumstances were right. Then I quit drinking for those two years, and later Jerry was Vice President, and then President, and I was too busy—and too much on display—to drink any appreciable amount.

In Rancho Mirage, the circumstances were right again.

We were staying in a leased house while our own new house was being built, and I started working on my autobiography. The constant pain in my neck and back made it unpleasant for me to get up or get dressed or exercise, but somehow I got through the spring and summer of 1977. You can reminisce lying down, if you need to.

At the same time I was collaborating with a writer on my book, I was collaborating with a decorator on fabrics and colors and wallpapers for the new house. It was going up right next door to the house of Nicky and Leonard Firestone, who were close to us in more ways than one.

Nicky wanted me to go see a doctor at USC who had helped one of her daughters with a knee problem; she thought he might be able to do something about my neck. She made the arrangements, I went to see the man, he ran tests and then phoned Nicky. "I'd be glad to treat Mrs. Ford," he said, "but until I could detox her from all these drugs she's taking, I couldn't do a thing."

He didn't say it to me, he said it to Nicky, and she never told me until much later.

As usual, nobody was telling me anything. They were afraid I *needed* all those drugs. So I went on having pain and taking pills. And feeling guiltless. Pills are infinitely preferable to alcohol if you're trying to convince yourself you're an innocent victim. Doctors prescribe pills, you don't have that excuse with alcohol.

Though I still mixed my poisons. I'd read the labels on pill bottles that said, "Do not operate heavy equipment or use alcohol while taking this medication," and I didn't operate heavy equipment, so I was 50 percent of the way home. As for the rest of it, I thought, well, those labels are for people who don't know how to drink. That's how insane I was, I thought I knew how to drink.

In the fall of 1977, I made a trip to Russia.

I had been hired to narrate the *Nutcracker* ballet (Jerry and I had signed contracts with NBC that called for each of us to appear on a certain number of television programs), and Bob Barrett accompanied me to Moscow. It was only September—the show was to be aired at Christmastime—but it was already very cold in Russia. I slept with my fur coat over me, and if Barrett and I needed to confer, we sat in the bathroom. It was warmer there.

I remember being driven through town in a limousine, siren screaming, and it didn't matter whether pedestrians were in the road or not, they just had to scatter. I was in terror that we would hit somebody. If the indifference of our driver to the possible injuries of his fellow proletarians made me anxious, so did my assignment. It was fun to visit the ballet school, but sitting in a theater box with all those cameras directed at me was worrisome. I was not a professional, I had no idea how I was coming off, and our three directors—a Russian, a Frenchman and the NBC guy—spent hours yelling at each other. There was vituperation in several languages.

I'd sit for ages in that box, and when they excused me, I'd head for the ladies' room and take another pill. I could hardly read the cue cards, I was so scared.

When the *Nutcracker* was broadcast back home, the press called me "sloe-eyed and sleepy-tongued," and they were right. I was so overmedicated. I didn't read the notices myself—they were so bad nobody brought them to me, and I certainly didn't search for them. I did watch the tape. Once. I have never had the nerve to look at it again.

Only recently, I asked Jerry if he'd been embarrassed by my appearance. "I knew it wasn't up to what you could do," he said. "It was so slow and deliberate and sedated. But I never told you, because I loved you and I didn't want to hurt you and I didn't want to face the facts."

Wherever I went that fall, I was in a fog. Sometimes a euphoric fog, sometimes a depressed fog. Dolores Hope invited me to serve on the board of Eisenhower Hospital in Rancho Mirage and I faithfully attended meetings, but I didn't contribute a thing. Dolores, who chaired those meetings, says friends were "mumbling" about me. "You were kind of a zombie," she says.

As your physical ability to function deteriorates, you deteriorate in all ways. The synergistic effect of pills plus a drink or two can be tremendous. Dr. Pursch used to tell us at Long Beach, "The impact isn't two plus two equals four, it's two plus two equals twenty-two."

Jerry believes that Steve and Jack, our two bachelor sons, stopped coming down to spend weekends with us because of "the disagreeable atmosphere that existed."

I tell him I don't like his use of the word "disagreeable," it sounds as though we quarreled, which we didn't. All right, he says, let's say "strained." "Both of us made a big effort to appear to be happy and getting along, we didn't advertise our difficulties, but the atmosphere was strained."

One of the things that drove him crazy was how long it took me to get dressed. I was like a record being played at the wrong speed. Nicky Firestone stopped asking me to lunch because I ate so slowly the other guests got tired of sitting there while I worked my way through a first course. Nicky said it could take me an hour to finish half a sandwich.

It was probably a relief to everybody when I started saying no to invitations. Sometimes Jerry did it for me. "I'd tell people you had the flu," he says. "I was making all these excuses an enabler does. It wasn't that you couldn't go because you were drunk, it was because you weren't healthy; you'd lost your enthusiasm for going to dinner or anywhere else."

I, a controller who had wanted to run the world, was so tranquilized I had become totally passive. Unless I got upset, and then I was very vocal. I was terribly sensitive, easily hurt. If

42

somebody said anything critical to me, I was shattered. I knew nobody liked me, and why should they? Inside, I was empty.

But every week without fail, I went to the doctor's office to be weighed, measured and given a B$_{12}$ shot. And every week I was making progress in the wrong direction, getting thinner, weaker, canceling myself out.

Then Christmas came, and my family got together and decided Something Has to Be Done about Mother.

The funny thing is that in the three months between Christmas and the intervention, I was more energetic and effectual than I had been in ages. I came back to Rancho Mirage from Vail and proceeded to get our new house ready to move into.

Even though I was sick, I was excited. I'd never owned a house in California before, I'd never had a decorator before ("All I knew was you liked green and white and blue," she says, "and that's what you got"), and as I mentioned earlier, I hadn't had new furniture in thirty years.

Everything was still a mess, the beds weren't in—I'm not sure the bedrooms were—and Jerry was traveling most of the time, and then we lost our lease on the house we'd been renting, so I had to spend the night wherever opportunity presented itself. I stayed at the Firestones' until their kids came for a visit, then I moved over to Susan's condo, but I couldn't stand her cat. Every night, that cat would come in and wrap itself around my neck, and I couldn't sleep. So I moved up to one of the golf cottages at Thunderbird Country Club. My code name (the name used by the Secret Service) has always been Pinafore, but the agents took to calling me Gypsy.

Every morning at six o'clock, I got up and went to the new house and unpacked. We had three huge moving vans filled with possessions from our house in Grand Rapids, possessions from our house in Virginia and personal things we had taken to the White House, all of which had been sitting in storage.

There was no organization, it was awful. Caroline Coventry helped me, and Clara was there at the very end, and we tore through boxes, me saying, "I want this in the study," or "This goes in the living room." I was determined to be finished before the fifteenth of March, when Jerry came home.

We had no space for half the stuff we unearthed. We piled it in the driveway, the garage. The dining room was solid with boxes—luckily, we still had no dining-room furniture—and the pool was just a big hole in the ground.

But we got the place into good enough shape so we could at least camp out there.

And two weeks after we moved in, they did the intervention. I kid Susan about it. "You waited till I got the whole job done, and then you sent me off to the hospital. Don't you have a twinge of guilt?" Susan says no. "You needed to go. You were sick."

I was sick. It took me sixty years to get to Long Beach, and every one of those years was deeply instructive. It was my life, I probably could not have done it another way, and nobody else was responsible for it. But now I had to change. Or die.

There's a saying among alcoholics that goes, you can take a bottle away from a man a thousand times, but he only has to put it down once.

At Long Beach, I would learn to put all my bottles down.

4

Extreme remedies are very appropriate for extreme diseases.

Hippocrates

Pat Benedict tells me I fell asleep on the way to Long Beach. She was saying it was a real pretty drive, the sun was shining, but I wasn't very excited about it. I had a lot of anxiety, and sleep was an escape. (Joe Pursch says I slept because I was denying my alcoholism, and he's a psychiatrist, but I have never understood what that had to do with it.)

As we drove onto the hospital grounds, there were cameramen taking pictures, and that upset me. I remember looking out the window of the car and thinking, I'm just not going to show them that I see them. I wondered how they knew I was coming, and I was ready to blame Pat or Pursch or the hospital, and I thought, they're waiting for me to issue a public statement, and I'm not sure I'm going to do it.

Dr. Pursch: "I knew getting her into the hospital would involve security and agents and telephone lines. And I also knew that alcoholism treatment is not like broken leg treatment, it has to involve other people. And when a group is meeting, for therapy, the door has to be closed. You can't have a Secret Service guy sitting in the group there with a big gun under his coat, and I knew she couldn't have what she normally had, a private room, a room for all the flowers people send, a room for her secretary.

"I believe you have to treat VIPs like any other patients, so there were no officers wearing their medals to greet her when she arrived, as there had been at Bethesda, when her husband was President. And I think this frosted her. She walked in like any other woman would, came up in the elevator, and stepped out into the hall."

And I almost turned right around and got back into the elevator. Because there in the hall was this huge sign that said "Alcohol Rehabilitation Center." I was not ready for that. I had a pill problem, was my position, don't make it sound worse than it is.

I balked at the sign, and I balked at the room they had put me in. There were four beds in that room.

Dr. Pursch: "Pat Benedict came running into my office and said, 'Oh, Captain, that nice lady has turned mad on you, she is going to leave, she won't even sit down.'

"I went into the room, and the nice lady was sitting down, but very straight, on a hard-backed chair. She had this little press release all coiled up in her fist like a diploma—it was going to tell the world why she was here—and she glared at me. 'I am accustomed to having a private room, Doctor,' she said. 'I have been in hospitals before, I'm a good patient, I do what doctors tell me, but not in this setting. Furthermore, you cannot have my statement, I will not release it.'

"I said, 'If you persist in isolation, I am going to tell the other three ladies you don't want to be with them, and they will have to move out.' I knew she couldn't permit me to move her roommates someplace else."

I had the paper with my statement on it—it had been written by my husband, Bob Barrett and me—and I threatened Dr. Pursch. I didn't want to go into a four-bed room. I thought the least they could do was give me a two-bed room. But he stood his ground. Poor Pat just wanted to fade into the background; she says I was very tough.

But Pursch called my bluff. "I'll have the other women come and get their things," he said, and I said, "Oh, no, you're not going to make anyone move for me," and with that, it was settled. I took the bed that was free.

(In each building of the Betty Ford Center, there is a four-bed room. Its occupants refer to it as the Swamp, supposedly in honor of my stay at Long Beach. And it's amazing how some of the people who need it most end up there; it's not a matter of assignment, either, it's just the luck of the draw. We had one very self-important woman arrive from New York—she announced she was a politician's wife, she wasn't going to stay, she was going straight home, she would not be stuck in any four-bed room. She was pretty loaded when she arrived, and giving the admissions people hell, and I said to John Schwarzlose, "If you want me to, I'll be glad to talk to her. I'll say, 'I know how you feel, but being in a four-bed room can be a great learning experience. And if I, coming from the White House, could manage it, I'll bet you can manage it too.'" I never had to do it. Apparently, the lady rethought her position, and showed up for breakfast the next morning mild as milk.)

My Long Beach roommates had been told I was to be treated just like anybody else, which was only sensible. A couple of them were young, regular Navy. There was one girl who had joined the Navy at eighteen, hadn't been in long, and was shipped home from overseas because she had such a severe drinking problem. She was very lonely. She used to sit on her bed a lot, and was difficult to get to know. She wouldn't open up even to the extent that I would. The third woman was older, much closer to my age. She was an admiral's wife and had been a recovering alcoholic. She'd gone for some root canal work, the dentist had given her Valium, she'd become addicted to Valium, and started drinking again.

Alcoholism is a chronic disease. You'll hear people say, "I was cured," but they're never cured. Alcoholism is treatable, but not curable. And it's progressive. You can abstain for forty years, and

47

if you start drinking again, it's as though you had been drinking all those years. You will become more desperately alcoholic more quickly.

I was not a model patient at Long Beach. I had a bit of the celebrity hang-up. I considered myself a very special person who had been married to a President of the United States, and I didn't think I should have to discuss my personal problems with just anybody. So group therapy was difficult for me. It was beneficial to me to hear the other people. I related to the feelings they were expressing, but I couldn't let anyone know *I* felt that way.

Dr. Pursch: "On the ward, the other patients were kind of tentative, watching to see how this President's wife was going to react, and she blended in very nicely. Forty-five minutes before she arrived, I had called all the patients together and told them a VIP would be coming in. I gave them a quick lecture on the VIP syndrome. I said it was their chance to be human, and to see that this otherwise privileged lady got at least an ordinary person's advantage. I said, if we treat this lady as somebody other than ourselves, she won't get well. So even though she has lived in the White House, she will be here on a first-name basis, as someone who has an illness, just like the rest of you.

"I said I also don't want any of you to call your wives whom you haven't talked to for six weeks because all of a sudden you have something to say. And I said, you counselors, I don't want to see that all of a sudden your wives have to come to the hospital to have lunch with you. The food is lousy. Am I making myself clear? I said I was going to be around all day, and the first man or woman that behaved like a schmuck would hear about it from me. Then I said, let's go about our business."

I don't remember much about treatment, but how could I? I was still sick. They told me it would be more than two years before I was completely free of all the chemicals I had used. Prescription drugs are much worse than alcohol that way, they have a very long half-life. So I would sit through lots of lectures and meetings and groups just listening, and trying to pick up one little thing that might make sense to me.

Most treatment programs are fairly simple, but it takes a smart person to work one. In the beginning of my sobriety, for instance, I had no idea what "let go and let God," meant. It's only five words, and I understand it very well today, but at that time, I was directing God, telling Him what *I* wanted. I probably gave Him a list.

At Long Beach—as at the Betty Ford Center, and Hazelden, and most good rehab places—patients are required to work the twelve steps of Alcoholics Anonymous. Also at Long Beach, we were required to go to an AA meeting every night. Anyone can go to an open AA meeting, you don't even have to be an alcoholic. Closed meetings are for alcoholics only. It was enough to make me punchy, but I guess I'd been punchy for some time. Meri Bell, whom Dr. Cruse had brought to meet me the week before I came to Long Beach, indicates as much.

Meri Bell Sharbutt: "The first time I saw her, her lips were quivering. She was terrified. She was very gracious, very polite, which you expect a public figure to be, and I talked to her and I talked to the family and then I wrote her a letter. Because when you're afraid, when you're in pain, it's hard to remember things that are said. You remember the gist, you remember the hope, but not the details.

"And the thing I wanted her clearly to understand was that I had been brought into her life because of a mutual disease. I was not a social climber. I said, 'We travel in different circles, our mutual alcoholism is the only thing we can build on. If friendship develops, that's one of the graces we receive. But it need not, it really need not. If you want to live, I am with you to the ends of the earth; if you want to drink, drink on your own time, don't talk to me.' "

It was Dr. Pursch who brought Muriel Zink into my life. He asked her to visit me at Long Beach because she was not only a

49

recovering alcoholic but very well known in the alcoholic rehabilitation field.

Muriel Zink: "I have a feeling Dr. Pursch had some other
women come in to meet her before me, but she and I just happened to click. I think he was not getting through to her completely on some levels, and he needed to bring in someone with
whom she could identify. We didn't talk so much about alcoholism the first time we met. I told her a little bit about myself, and I
didn't ask too many questions.

"I knew it had been Susan who had blown the whistle on her,
and I told her about my own daughter. She said she had once
been able to silence Susan with just a look, but this time, Susan
had persisted, and how hurtful it had been. We talked a little bit
about intervention. After I left her that first day, I did a lot of soul-
searching about whether I really did connect that much with her
and did I really think she was that neat, or was it because of who
she was. Was it that I liked the reflected glory? And I decided as
long as I was being myself, and not trying to impress, it was okay.

"Later I got a call from Dr. Pursch saying, 'Mrs. Ford really
enjoyed her visit with you. I wonder if you could come back
down again?' And I said sure. And he said, 'Listen, would it be
possible to bring a women's meeting over here to her? Because
the meeting here has swelled considerably since she's come, and
I think a smaller group would be helpful.'

"So we came, about fourteen women, and we held a meeting. She was gracious, like a hostess, distributing and picking up
the ashtrays. She was not terribly self-disclosing. After that, she
came to my home in Laguna for a women's meeting, and we took
meetings to her in Long Beach again. She has since said that the
support of these women meant a lot to her.

"Now she talks so easily about her alcoholism, she can say
'drunk,' she's down-to-earth and specific, but back then she had
to use euphemisms, explain that her medications had been prescribed by a doctor. She couldn't say, 'I am an addict.' But I don't
think that's unusual. I believe as time goes by you begin to under-

50

stand more, and see more clearly, and identify yourself more with others."

I really liked Muriel, and I wanted to hear what she had to say. I wanted to listen. I'm sure I didn't want to talk to her, I didn't want to talk to anybody, but I thought she was a classy lady, and would be a nifty friend, and if they wanted me to get acquainted with somebody, she was the somebody I was going to pick. She was not threatening. I didn't feel she looked down on me. The first thing she said to me was "You're unique, but you're not unique." I had been a President's wife, but I was also a woman like her, we both had daughters, she came across warm and friendly.

All the women in that support group did. I will be forever grateful to them; they drove an hour from Laguna to Long Beach, and an hour back, just to meet with me once a week, and each one talked about her recovery, and the things she had done in denial of her alcoholism. When I heard one who was president of some Republican women's group say she had always laced her coffee with vodka on the bad days, I thought of myself back in Virginia, and knew, even if I wasn't ready to admit it, I was like that woman under the skin.

Muriel is right that I wouldn't say I was a drunk. That was beginning to bother a lot of them at Long Beach. Including Dr. Pursch.

I've thought about this a lot. I could *not* say I was alcoholic. I didn't relate to any of the drunk stories I heard. I had never had an urge to hang out at bars, I wasn't about to get kicked out of the Navy if I didn't shape up, nobody was suing me for running over their cat while under the influence.

I knew there was something wrong with me, or my family wouldn't have done the intervention. But there's an enormous difference between other people's thinking you're alcoholic and your thinking you're alcoholic. I was perfectly happy not to drink, I wasn't making a big deal out of not drinking, I was longing for pills, not Pilsener.

I kept asking for medication, and they wouldn't give it to me.

51

I complained that my arm and neck were bothering me. It didn't do me a bit of good. They wanted me to exercise. Well, I was too old and too fragile to play volleyball with the rest of them, but I had a physical therapy program, and I had a walking program. I learned to walk a mile in fourteen minutes. And it was pretty bleak walking—out to the baseball diamond and back. Because Long Beach is a city, all the views from the hospital were of office buildings, empty lots and traffic, and the weather was sad and overcast that April.

We all wore name tags, and wherever I walked, the sailors would yell out, "Hi, Betty." I was sixty, and certainly the oldest patient there at the time. In spite of the fact that they were supposed to treat me normally, I sort of became a pet.

In a sense, I was like a child born into recovery with a gold spoon in its mouth. How could I fail? I had the whole country behind me. Sailors, family, friends, even the press. Not everybody in such a situation gets that kind of support.

When I went into treatment, I was a very slow learner. I said the things I was supposed to say, but no great light went on in my brain. Example: It was suggested to us patients that a power greater than ourselves could restore us to "sanity." I took offense at that. My first reaction was, well, these people must be much worse off than I am, because I certainly am not insane, and never have been. The idea that you didn't have to be insane to commit an insane act—like insisting on driving while drunk—didn't register with me.

I didn't understand about "self-honesty" either. Wasn't I as honest as the day is long? When I was a child, and charged penny candy on the grocery bill, hadn't I come downstairs that very night and told my mother about it because it was on my conscience? And hadn't she spanked me for it? I never forgave her, and it was a wonder I was ever honest again, but I was. When my counselor talked to me about getting honest with myself, I thought, what the hell does he mean?

But at least I listened. I knew I'd better listen, because I hadn't done a very good job on my own. There's a saying you hear in recovery, "Bring the body, and the mind will follow." I brought the body and wondered if the mind would ever understand.

Then something horrible happened. It was about ten days into my treatment. I'd been in my regular therapy group, Group Six—we called ourselves the Six-Pack—and I'd thought we had an excellent session. My notes say, "Really good meeting. Dr. Lew's thoughts about the First, Second and Third steps. . . . A discussion of Jim's problem last night. He was curled up crying. Things are really moving along, with everyone openly sharing." Except, probably, me.

Anyway, after our individual small groups broke up, there was a big meeting of all the groups. Jerry was there that day, and went to the meeting with me, and Joe Cruse spoke, and I was pleased to see him.

Lunch followed, and then Jerry and I were summoned to Dr. Pursch's office. There were Pursch, Cruse, Pat Benedict, my counselor and another doctor.

Dr. Cruse: "Pursch had noticed that Betty was getting a little cocksure, she had begun to pull back and get into her denial again, she wasn't as bad off as a lot of the sailors and wives and so forth. That's what the disease does. So he called me to come over, and the President and Pat and Betty's counselor were there, and we just sort of redid the intervention. That's the first time she really broke down and sobbed, rather than crying silent tears as she had in the first intervention."

Dr. Pursch: "She was scared and angry and frightened and puzzled. She was hoping to continue to reserve for herself the right not only to drink but not to be labeled a drunk. I said, 'We are here because something needs to be faced, and that is that you are also dependent on alcohol.' The President said nothing, and Betty said, 'If you're going to call me an alcoholic, I won't stand for it.'

"I said, 'So far, you have only talked about drugs, but you are going to have to make a public statement saying you are also dependent on alcohol.' She said, 'I can't do that, I don't want to embarrass my husband.'

"I said, 'You are hiding behind your husband, and if you don't believe it, ask him.' And she kind of looked over at the President and said, 'Well?' And he said, 'No, you won't embarrass me.' She was hyperventilating, flushing, blanching, flushing, her blood vessels were going crazy."

Pat Benedict: "I had not been allowed to spend much time with Betty at Long Beach because Dr. Pursch wanted to transfer her dependence 'from one person to a group, an idea, a system.'

"Treatment was out of my realm, anyway. I had been asked to take her to the women's meeting at Laguna—in order to protect her privacy, we went through a back alley to get there—and I remember saying, 'Betty, before I met you, I used to walk in the front door of these places,' and she laughed and said, 'Well, you hang around me, you've got to go through the alleys.'

"I was still on chemotherapy—I'd only had my mastectomy a few months before—and I was sick in bed on the morning when Dr. Pursch's secretary phoned and said he wanted me in his office at one o'clock. I said, 'I can't.' She said, 'He wants you there.' So I got up and put on a pair of slacks and went over.

"Pursch confronted Betty on her alcoholism, and he was kind of ruthless. I was sitting next to her, and I remember her little eyes were filling, her little nose was running, and I put my arm around her and just held her. They didn't want her to get over pills and keep drinking, and that's how Pursch does things, but I thought, damn you, this is kind of like being raped. It was very hard on her because he isn't tender. To me, that second intervention was the more painful, and of course, I had grown to love her very much."

Jerry Ford: "Pursch was very tough. I think he felt Betty wasn't responding, she was in denial, she had probably been trying to shut herself off, and he thought he had to shock her. I thought she was going to stomp out of that office. She was mad as hell. I don't remember what I said except that I never considered embarrassment a problem. I never felt any embarrassment, period. Afterward, I got her back to her room, and she lay down. She was still in tears, and I tried to console her, encourage her, strengthen her resolve."

I probably wasn't having anything to do with him at that point. I was real mad and hurt that he hadn't spoken up to defend me. He hadn't allowed me the out I was looking for. I had cried so hard my nose and ears were closed up, my head felt like a balloon, all swollen. Jerry called a doctor to come listen to my chest, and after a while I simmered down. I think it was more the way Pursch did it than what he did. Maybe he should just have said, "Well, Betty, you hide. You're very alcoholic, but it's hidden in your sickness. You hide behind it, you lean on your back or your neck or something."

I don't know, that might have infuriated me just as much. The thing he said that really made me mad was "Betty, you're just as alcoholic as anyone can be, and you're using your husband to hide behind."

I didn't believe I was alcoholic for a minute and I certainly wasn't hiding behind my husband, but I finally figured, if that's what they wanted me to say, then I would say it. If I made enough Brownie points, maybe they'd let me go home early.

They gave another statement to the press the next day. I wrote it out in longhand, and my husband added a couple of corrections. It said in part, "Due to the excellent treatment I have had here at the Long Beach Naval Hospital, I have found I am not only addicted to the medication I have been taking for my arthritis, but also to alcohol. So I am grateful for this program of recovery . . . and pleased to have the opportunity to attend it. I expect it to be a solution for my problems."

What I expected—or hoped—was now they'd all get off my back.

I kept a kind of diary—not regularly, but from time to time— at Long Beach. Here are a couple of entries:

55

April 21: "Phone call from Jerry. He filled me in on the progress of the house, new driveway, office, etc. Now to bed. Hell, these damned scratchy blankets. Little did I know when I signed in here it was going to be so rough. It's a good program, but mighty hard for anyone 20, let alone someone who was 60 two weeks ago. Two weeks into my sobriety. Oh well, just one week more, and I get a weekend pass. What in the hell am I doing here? I've even started to talk like the sailors, but I can't sign out. I want it too badly, guess I'll just cry."

April 28: "Hurray. I go home for the weekend. What a relief. Jerry will be there tonight. Now just to get through the day— reveille, breakfast, muster, group, lecture, meetings, physical therapy, lunch."

Jerry Ford: "At the end of three weeks, she came home for a weekend, and there was a tremendous difference. She was just a totally different person."

One part of this totally different person was not entirely adorable. I was on a short string, my nerves were raw, only three weeks into treatment. People don't understand the mood swings of a recovering alcoholic. I went to the beauty parlor, and the operator cut my hair very short, and I didn't realize what was happening until one side was finished. "What are you doing?" I asked. She said, "Oh, Caroline told me you wanted it short so you could swim in the pool."

I went home with blood in my eye, and screamed at Caroline Coventry, "I could kill you for doing this to me!" I really carried on. Luckily she was as much friend as secretary, and a diplomat to boot.

(I remember back one time when I was making a speech and Caroline said, "Mrs. Ford, please don't take your pills until after you get through with your remarks, because I notice sometimes you don't sound as believable or real as you could." She was trying to be delicate, so she didn't come right out and say you're tripping over your tongue. Friends and family protected me from self-knowledge even as I protected myself. I think this is what happens. You develop a shell that prevents anyone's seeing your true self. You work so hard to prevent anyone else from seeing it that pretty soon you don't see it either.)

On that weekend at home, I was struck by how beautiful everything was. Our decorator, Laura Mako, had done a marvelous job, the dining room was finished, the pool and the Jacuzzi ready, the fountains going. All in three weeks.

On Saturday morning, Dr. Cruse came by to check my blood pressure, and I did some brooding over one of my mates in the Six-Pack, a guy named Hal. You might think I had enough to do, dealing with my own inadequacies, but I was crazy about Hal, and he seemed to be doing all the right things, he spouted the vocabulary, he'd been in treatment before, yet Pat thought he was going to drink again. (Indeed, he did drink again on his way home from Long Beach.)

The most obvious reason you worry about your teammates, aside from affection, is that they mirror your own recovery; if they can't make it, how will you be able to?

For my fourth and final week of treatment, I came back to Long Beach with a box of Kleenex, some Lipton's tea and some quarters for the soda machine.

That last week, I was much more active in my group. During the first days, I had acted as an observer; I had a measure of disdain for the people who didn't speak up so I could listen and learn. Because *I* didn't want to speak up, I liked those who did, who were open and aggressive and up-front and had lots to say. The more they told their colorful stories, the more they kept the focus off me. I was scornful of the ones who hung back. I thought, they just don't want to admit they've got this problem. Yet I didn't identify myself as one of them.

Nobody ever yelled at me, or said *you're* hanging back, not even the counselor. Maybe they were a little afraid to do it to me, maybe I had them conned. I was a pretty good con artist.

Though sometimes you're not quite so clever as you think. I remember in the Laguna women's group announcing that I never drank much, just a little bit, socially, and they all kept perfectly straight faces and said, "That's right, that's what I

57

thought too, until I began to get well." They were kind, but they weren't conned.

To step back a bit, it was in my second week at Long Beach that I was finally shocked into admitting to my peer group that I was alcoholic. It happened at a family session where a young woman got up and said she didn't know why her family was making such a big deal about her drinking. The family sessions were much more open than, say, the Six-Pack sessions. Doctors could walk into them, so could any family members. My husband and Steve and Susan all took some family therapy while I was at Long Beach.

"My drinking hasn't caused my folks any trouble," this girl said. And I was well aware that her drinking had caused her folks a lot of trouble, and it was my turn to speak next and suddenly I was on my feet, and I said, "I'm Betty, and I'm an alcoholic, and I *know* my drinking has hurt my family." Because I thought, by God, if she isn't gutsy enough to say it, I will.

It surprised me to hear myself and yet it was a relief.

I had some trouble relating to the very young sailors—men or women. There was one little girl, just a peewee in size and age, and she talked about sniffing crankcase grease to get high, and I had never heard of anything like that, I only related to nice social settings with lovely tall crystal glasses.

And pills. One of my fellow inmates for whom I felt particular sympathy was a young doctor from Bethesda. Before he came to Long Beach, he'd been writing himself narcotics prescriptions, and having them filled all over a sixty-mile area, and he knew he was getting down to the line, that pretty soon the authorities were going to catch up with those numbers on his prescription pads.

Being in there with all those Navy men made me think about my brother Bob. During World War II, he'd served in the South Pacific cleaning out Japanese machine-gun nests, and he came home not only a hero but an alcoholic. Yet he managed to sober up and go on to help a lot of other drunks. At his funeral, my brother Bill and I were moved by the numbers of people who showed up just to express their love for Bob. "That church was absolutely filled," Bill says, "with poor Indians and ministers and people that flew in on their Lear jets."

In the end, whether or not I could identify with the habits of a twenty-year-old mechanic who'd gone around slurping up the dregs out of grown-ups' glasses since he was eight years old, I could identify with his disease. We were all suffering from the same thing, and it didn't matter where we came from or how we got here. If we could have done something about our sickness on our own, we'd have done it, and stayed out there where the rest of the people are. We stay out there a long time anyway, because that's where we think the fun is. It's one of the reasons recovery is so slow.

So we had a lot in common, and we began to listen to each other, and examine our mutual puzzlement. Because most of us *were* puzzled. We didn't know how we got here, we didn't plot our lives so that at seventeen, or twenty-three, or sixty, we could go into treatment. It isn't like setting your sights on a trip around the world.

But we helped each other in countless ways. And we laughed a lot while we were at it. There was a game called Lifeboat—very psychologically revealing, I'm sure—where a bunch of us were supposed to be in a lifeboat together, and the boat was going to sink unless a couple of people got out. You had to justify being allowed to stay on board. After we'd heard from everybody, we voted on which unfortunates to jettison.

Some people were noble, and announced that they should be the ones to go because they were the heaviest, or the oldest, or the most useless. Others, with more survival instinct, hung on and justified their presence.

I was one of those. I said, "As long as you have me on board, the Secret Service will keep looking till they find us." Not nice? Never mind, the Bloomers are tough.

During our free time—of which there was not a great deal— there were card games, and kibitzing of card games, and drinking of coffee. We all ate together in a cafeteria on the ground level in back. We read, we tried to answer our mail.

I got lots. Not only asking for help, but offering help—under-

59

standing, encouragement, praise. I appreciated people's caring, but was astonished at the amount of newspaper coverage, the editorials commending my heroism, my candor, my courage. I hadn't rescued anybody from a burning building, I'd simply put my bottles down. It was my family, not I, who had been "candid" and "courageous."

Dr. Pursch says he got calls all day long from reporters who said, "I know she's dying to talk to me, and they won't let me get to her." There was even one TV crew that rented a bread truck and drove in and opened the truck's doors, and a TV camera started taking pictures.

I was still telling myself—foolishly, perhaps—that even if I'd gone public with my alcoholism, my recovery was a private matter. Or at least a matter between me and my family and my doctors and my fellow patients. Which got me into another mess.

I had finished my first book. It was already in galleys. And I didn't see any reason to go back and stick in a lot of stuff about alcoholism and drugs.

Dr. Pursch: "I used to talk to her in one-on-one sessions. I remember two incidents. One was the book. She was bragging to me—it must have been the first or second day of her stay at Long Beach—about it. She said, 'My book is coming out,' and of course I'd heard about it. I said, 'What do you mean, it's coming out?' She said, 'I just told you, it's finished.' I said, 'Yeah, but is it complete?' And she looked at me like, God, this guy doesn't talk English good.

"There was another thing like that a couple of weeks later that may not sound as though it related to the book, but it did. I had brought her a little audiotape. It was of a famous politician giving a talk on alcoholism at some meeting or convention. He was then seven years sober. She pushed the tape back at me and said, 'You might as well know, I will never do stuff like that, so don't count on my running around the country talking about how I am an alcoholic.'

"She was still too proud, she couldn't go back on her image, she was saying, don't push me into public view."

I wasn't ready to talk about my alcoholism or my drug addiction. I was having a hard enough time addressing it myself.

When the publishers said a chapter on Long Beach had to go into the book, I said, "No, I won't do it, it has nothing to do with the book."

Jerry Ford: "If my recollection is accurate, it was a crisis. The publishers were uptight, and we had to very delicately convince Betty that it was a proper conclusion to *The Times of My Life.* There was no other responsible way to end the book. I felt the request of the publishers was legitimate, and the problem was to prevail on Betty, make her believe that she could, in her early recovery, be forthright and go public."

Dr. Pursch: "She had physically become very small, and crumpled into herself, but mentally, she was undiminished, and she had the same problems many intelligent people have, she had some anger at existential forces, the fickle finger of fate. Why does this have to happen to me? What did I do? I was no worse than a lot of people I know. But she didn't have the ego slippage —in a psychiatric sense—where she lost track of conversations or she couldn't remember things. And she had a kind of interesting clinical stubbornness. She wanted to make sure that nobody would subvert her or take over her life."

In the instance of my book, my stubbornness was to no avail. I finally had to agree to add a kind of postscript to my story, and at this point, I can say I am glad I *didn't* win the argument. Too many people have written to tell me how that brief chapter gave them the courage to go for help.

As for my ability to remember conversations, I'm not so sure about that, but I am single-minded. Laura Mako says when we were choosing furniture and fabrics, there were times when I would take my little pill, and drift off, and she'd sit there and wait for me to come back. And some days, she would have to go over the same ground she'd traveled the day before, but she says,

"You'd pick the same thing all over again. You had a one-track mind."

It wasn't so much that I knew what I was doing as that I knew what I wanted.

I have been asked how my family feels now that they can't control me anymore, when I'm no longer this nice dopey pill pusher, sitting around nodding. Well, Jerry says they couldn't control me *then*, that in my weakness, my sickness, whatever you want to call it, I controlled everyone. They were all out there fronting for me, covering up, making excuses, and some of them were more resentful than others. Susan found out about her own anger when she came to Long Beach for that week of family therapy.

Susan Ford: "Dad was there for a while, and when he left I went and took his place in a small group. Pete was my counselor. You kind of go in and tell your story, and Dad had taken credit for getting the intervention together, and I was absolutely furious. I said, 'No way. I did it. I'm the one who put the pieces together. Without him, I couldn't have done it, but where does he get off taking all the credit?' Getting that off my chest was a good experience.

"Then one morning, for some reason, nobody wanted to talk, so Pete read us a short story called 'Warm Fuzzies.' It was something about how somebody took a warm fuzzy away from somebody. Well, it was like taking my heart and pulling it out, it was like the way I felt about my mother, and how she had taken everything away from me, I never had a chance to be a kid, I was always covering for her, and was it really fair, and when was it going to be my turn? That sort of thing. And nobody wanted to comment. And Pete finally said, 'Hey, guys, Susan is asking for help, and nobody wants to say anything.' And then everybody started talking and it was fine. It really made me feel so much better."

Steve Ford: "I was scared to come around at first. I was pretty young, and once Mom got to the naval hospital, I had the sort of feeling that, okay, the doctor's got her under control, and I'll give her some calls and stuff, but I don't need to show up there. Pat Benedict and some other people reassured me that I did need to go up there, that it was important, and I shouldn't be scared, it was part of growing.

"I'll never forget one group session. They talked about if your parents were alcoholic, then it was very likely that you could become alcoholic, and I made the dumb statement, 'Oh, no, I'll never be an alcoholic'—you know, when you're twenty, you think you know everything—and they jumped all over me. 'Do you think your mother decided to be an alcoholic?' And I had to accept it, yes, I have a good chance of becoming alcoholic, because of my family background.

"The thing I remember best about Long Beach is that Mom was treated like everybody else. She had been First Lady, and that was part of the problem. Her doctors would prescribe whatever she wanted, because they didn't want to make a First Lady mad.

"When I came to Long Beach for the first time, I went down to the cafeteria, where Mom was having something to eat with some of the boys, and they were telling off-color jokes, and I was a little offended. I thought, hey, what is this? Guys telling off-color jokes to my mom here, the First Lady?

"There were admirals and seamen all mixed up, and they were telling these jokes, and she was laughing and having a good time. And it wasn't till later that I realized she needed to be in a real world where people didn't care who she was. That was one of the most important things to come out of Long Beach. It got her back in touch with what people are all about."

Jerry Ford: "I was in a group of five or six who were recovering alcoholics. I spent about five days in all. And I went to a number of meetings with Betty. For the first time I learned about alcoholism. Its being a disease. I saw officers and seamen in my group, and they all had alcohol problems. I went to lectures with fifty or a hundred patients and their families, co-dependents like me.

"It was very educational. I learned that I was making all these excuses an enabler does."

When you have four weeks in a recovery program, your first goal is sobriety. And then you have to find reasons to *stay* sober. I feel better, my life is better, drinking doesn't fix my problems. You say the words, but your understanding is far from perfect.

The body recovers first. As I became freer of the drugs, even my skin began to tingle. The shock of feeling all this is rather disconcerting; your physical body is coming alive again just as the emotions you had medicated away come alive too.

When I first got to Long Beach, I was so shaky I couldn't go down the hall to get coffee. And they wouldn't even let me take vitamins in pill form, they made me take them in a powder I could shake on my cereal.

But treatment, whatever length it may be, is just that first good swift kick in the pants that's supposed to get you back on the track a little bit.

True sobriety is built more slowly. True sobriety is freedom, and not having to white-knuckle it twenty-four hours a day, worrying that you may drink, or use.

True sobriety is living by a program that helps you handle your emotions so they don't get you in trouble. I was a long way from there when I went home.

But I was sober, and I was beginning to eat right, and exercise. And I was beginning to be happy again.

5

Heaviness may endure for a night,
but Joy cometh in the morning.
The Book of Common Prayer

I said in the preface to this book that there is joy in recovery.
Right from the beginning.

I was on a high because my life was all coming together,
everybody was happy with me, I'd gone and done something
about my alcoholism and drug dependency, I was the apple of
everyone's eye.

It didn't stay that way. I had to prepare myself for reality.
There would be dips in that happiness, there would be, from time
to time, anger. There would be many adjustments.

I thought I had it made, and the truth was, I didn't have it
made at all, I had only taken the first step. It was a big step, but
the trip was only beginning. At first, the euphoria was enough. I
think of myself numbed by so many drugs I can't even remember
their names. I had been flat for so long I hadn't heard much of
anything, and here I was, body and brain coming alive again.

I began to see the world I'd just been walking through,
sleeping through. For me now, there was joy in waking up in the
morning, just being able to put my two feet on the floor and go
where I wanted to go, even with a bad neck and a bad back and
all the rest of it.

I was grateful. I had friends who were dead. From drinking, from cancer. I could have been, and I wasn't. And I had an ego that made me believe I was still young and competitive. Put me on the beach at Maui with a bunch of people in their forties, and they're body surfing, and I think, why shouldn't I body surf?

Body surfing is easy. It's working a recovery program that's hard. It's the reading, the studying, the going to peer group meetings. I had come home without any great enthusiasm for joining any support group. I figured, after my twenty-eight-day crash course, I didn't need to be in meetings every day of the week. And that was where Meri Bell came in.

I spoke to her every day. She didn't permit me to retreat into my old manipulative style of ducking out of whatever I didn't want to do. Jerry was helpful too. Sometimes I'd try to skip a night, and he'd say, "You always feel better if you go," and I'd go, fuming a little, but I'd be glad later.

Meri Bell was a tiger. She glared at strangers who came near me in meetings. She was aggressive, protective, she said she didn't want my sobriety threatened by a lot of clamor.

It was my habit to be gracious to anyone who approached, but she said, "You're not here to play former First Lady, you're here for the same reason the rest of us are here, to stay sober and work the program to the best of your ability."

Meri Bell Sharbutt: "By the time Betty came back from Long Beach, I had already told a group of women with whom I was associated that a public figure would be coming into our group, and that she was alcoholic, just as I was, as they were. And that's why she was coming, and she should not be treated any differently than they would like to be treated, and if I saw anybody doing that, I would call them on it. I told the ones who were a little pushy, 'Don't treat her like a celebrity, help her find out what being an alcoholic means.'

"A lot of people put Betty on a pedestal. She couldn't stop that. But what she could do was not put herself on a pedestal. During that first year, she listened to me, and did not speak publicly about recovery. I said you ought not to speak of recovery

66

until you know what recovery is. There are people in the field who say, 'Oh, you can help so many people, you can do so much.' And you want to, and before you know it, you're drawn into this trap of talking glibly with head knowledge, but not heart experience. And there is a big, big difference.

"Betty is a public figure. She is acquainted with arthritis and cancer from personal knowledge. And now alcoholism. And whatever she says may be taken as gospel by a lot of people.

"The big secret, it seemed to me, was for her to keep quiet long enough to find out where she was going."

It was easy for me to keep quiet; speaking out was what terrified me. I used to go to meetings at the last minute to make sure no one would know I was going to be there, for fear they might call on me in some way. And then I got to this one beginners' meeting, and the leader said, "Betty," and like a dumbbell, in sheer panic, I spoke up and said, "Oh, yes, I'm Betty and I'm an alcoholic." And what I didn't know was there were several other Bettys in the room, and if I'd just kept my mouth shut, I wouldn't have had to speak.

Speaking is frightening not so much because you're uncomfortable talking, but because you're afraid you're going to make a fool of yourself by saying something stupid. And we all have this great wish to prove ourselves the brightest, most capable, most erudite. It's a terrible feeling when you join a new group and you don't really know them and they don't really know you. You're so unsure of yourself.

When we would read aloud from books on alcoholism, we'd go around a table, and each of us would take one paragraph. I'd be counting heads, trying to figure how many paragraphs before they would get to me. Of course, that meant I didn't hear anything that was going on; I was too busy rehearsing *my* part. Not only did I miss the whole point, I invariably got caught, because somebody would decide she didn't have her glasses, and she wanted to pass, and I'd be all prepared with the wrong paragraph.

I had to learn I was okay, that I didn't have to be perfect

67

before someone would like me, that it was even okay to be number two, like Avis, as long as I was trying harder.

For me, going to a beginners' meeting is special now. I realize that, after a few years of sobriety, I've forgotten those shaky, scary feelings, and it's good to be reminded of what it's like for the new people.

I went to a beginners' meeting a little while ago. There was a boy there who said he came from nothing, off the streets, but he wasn't drinking anymore, and he wasn't shooting up, and he felt good. "I'm working now," he said. "I never had anything before. If I had anything, I sold it to get drugs. Now I'm starting to buy things, and I just sit in my room and look at them. I got a disc player, I got a TV." He held up a wristwatch, and everyone cheered. "It isn't mine," he said. "I bought it for my girlfriend. I never bought anybody anything before. Except maybe a bottle of Thunderbird."

And then he said this great line. "If I was all there, I wouldn't be here. But I'm okay."

Clean and sober. The jubilation of it. There was a woman at that meeting who said she'd just got through the worst day she'd ever lived. Her car had broken down, her little girl had chicken pox, an old boyfriend she detested had shown up, fresh out of jail, on her doorstep. "But I didn't take a drink," she said. "And I didn't do a line. And I'm happy."

There was another young woman who was just out of treatment, and terrified to go to a shopping mall or a movie. She'd been okay in the treatment center, a protected place, but the world outside seemed too big and threatening. "So I came to this meeting," she said, "and it makes me feel whole."

Street kids, jet setters—alcoholics come from all walks of life. There was a foreign girl who had just finished a stint at a treatment center, and she made us all laugh. She said she'd been on holiday on the Riviera, and in the middle of a drink, she had set down her glass and gone to the phone and called the international operator and asked to be connected with the rehab. When she reached admissions, she asked how long treatment lasted.

She was told four to six weeks, and was appalled. "I can't stay forty-six weeks," she said.

A boy who was still in treatment at the BFC—we bus them to an outside group once a week—came up to me after the meeting. "I fight the program," he said. "I don't understand it. But in spite of myself, I'm coming back to life. When I was a kid, I talked a lot. Then, with the drugs, I drew back into myself."

"You'll talk again," I said. "I promise you."

The terrors of those first meetings, and the wonders of those first meetings. Once in a while, during the first year of my sobriety, I felt like a Martian. I sat on the sidelines and listened to young women punctuating their sentences with four-letter words, telling of making their bread on the streets, prostituting themselves to get drugs or alcohol or take care of babies whose fathers were gone.

I had come from such a different milieu; my experiences did not encompass slashing my wrists, or being rescued by the police after swallowing a bottle of whiskey and putting a gun in my mouth. I simply could not see any reflection of myself in those women. *I* wasn't suicidal. But the more I listened, the more I thought about it, the more I wondered, was I really so different?

I hadn't literally closed up the house, but inside myself, I had been pulling down the shades. It had been my form of suicide. It had been what I wanted.

In those rooms, amidst a sea of Styrofoam coffee cups and a fog of cigarette smoke, I began to understand that I did indeed share those women's disease. And their hopes.

In the beginning, you are more fragile than you—or other people—realize. I came home from Long Beach—they had cameras there to televise my leaving—and discovered I was on instant display. I had been twenty-eight days in treatment, I was still going through drug withdrawal, which takes one to two years, and I found I was expected to greet a lot of Republicans who were having a reception at my house. Not only that, but NBC was coming in to do an interview.

I broke down and cried, I begged not to have it happen. But the TV crew had already arrived from New York. Nobody had consulted me, nobody had consulted my doctors; it was typical leftover White House programming. There's going to be a television interview, we expect you to be ready. Finally, I agreed to sit in the study on the couch next to my husband, and the TV people asked me how I was, and I said I was just fine, gritting my teeth behind my smile.

To me, it was a cruel intrusion; it was as if they had bought a piece of my life that I had no intention of selling to them.

There was no way I should have been put under such pressure. I was upset with my husband, with politics, with everything and everybody. But something good came from that. Now when I talk to patients at the Center—and I often talk to patients and their families together—I say, 'Stay out of each other's way. You're all very fragile, it's too early to try to run each other's lives.' The person who has just gone through recovery is responsible for himself, and the family members have to realize they must stop trying to manage the alcoholic—who can't be managed anyway. That's terribly important.

In your fragility, you sometimes lose your sense of humor. The first summer after treatment, we were, as usual, in Vail, and since I couldn't have medication, I was taking hot showers, hot packs, electrical treatments for muscle spasms, and so forth. At one point, when I was lying on the hot packs, I saw a little mouse come out of a closet and run around the room and go behind the television set. I was worried he might hit a cable, get a shock, but he was fine; eventually, he ran back into his closet.

The first day I saw him, I didn't think much about it. We were up in the mountains, in the woods, and we had lots of critters there. Well, this little guy apparently went home and told his dear ones it was okay in my bedroom, and next day he came back with a girlfriend.

When I went in to lunch, I said to my husband and the caretaker, "Do you realize we've got mice? They come out of the closet, run across the room, behind the television, over the draperies, and then go back into the closet."

Jerry turned to the caretaker. "Jon," he said, "she must be drinking again."

70

I did keep my mouth shut, and was proud of myself. I thought, that's pretty good, I didn't jump down his throat in front of Jon. But later, when we were alone, I told him how I felt. "I know you're kidding," I said, "but you have no idea how raw my wounds are. So please, don't ever say anything like that to me again, particularly in front of someone else. Because it hurts."

P.S.: The next day, they set mousetraps. I was sorry to see the little fellows caught.

We're delicate in our recovery.

And we don't like to be patronized either. Sometimes, on an airplane, a flight attendant, knowing my history, will pick up my wineglass without even asking me whether or not I want wine. Early in my sobriety, that bothered me. The attendant is trying to be helpful, but it doesn't help at all. In fact, it's quite disturbing to someone newly sober who has been told, "It's your choice, you have the right to drink or not to drink, and only you can make that decision."

When I first came home from Long Beach, I just wanted to get on with my life. In my mind it was like, I've done what I was supposed to do, now let me enjoy my beautiful new bathroom with the sunken tub. I couldn't wait to use the swimming pool, I couldn't wait to entertain.

And we entertained a fair amount that year. We had guests from Washington who sat in the living room and said, "Betty, you just can't be alcoholic. Oh, sure, we all had a few drinks, but you always went home in good shape." Or, "Betty, you never had a problem. I never saw you when you were out of it." I had a lot of work to do, just to sit there and say, "I know you didn't see me when I was out of it." Because I had never allowed *anyone* to see me looking unladylike.

Jerry was no help either. He would say, "Well, you know she never had any trouble with alcohol until she got tangled up with those pills." This was dangerous stuff for me to hear. I had to turn it off and go back to my support groups. Because the voice of the siren, murmuring, "You were never an alcoholic," fed my own denial. I was like the girl who's a teeny bit pregnant. In my own head, if I was alcoholic, it was just the teeniest bit.

71

In the groups, they said, "Keep coming back," and, "It works." So I kept coming back, still thinking I wasn't exactly like them, but I had no place else to go.

Sometimes, at night, I would get into bed, and when my husband put his arms around me, I would dissolve. "I just don't understand how I could have done this to you and the children. I'm so ashamed." Jerry would be very calm, and say he was grateful that I was recovering, and alcoholism was a disease, it wasn't something I'd tried to go out and get.

The changes involved in coming home, the emotional relationships with your husband and your family, are difficult. Because all you have done so far is learn a little about your disease, and on sleepless nights you brood over how you've been away for treatment of something that has a stigma associated with it, and you wonder what people are thinking about you. You haven't yet learned to wonder, what am *I* thinking? I had so much guilt, I blamed myself so much, I badgered Meri Bell as well as Jerry. "I'm an intelligent woman, and I love my family. Why would I do a thing like this? Why would I disappoint them?"

And she would say I was an alcoholic, and if I had not been an alcoholic, then I probably would have been aware of the invisible line that you cross when you move from social drinking to alcoholic drinking. But how? If the line is invisible, how do you see it?

I would guess that I didn't really accept my alcoholism until I was almost a year in the program. But even though I thought I was different, I felt closeness with the other recovering people. All of us had known what it was like to have our lives out of control. In a little black book I treasure, I found a very important message. It said there are two days we don't have to worry about. One is yesterday, because it's gone, and we can't live it over. The other is tomorrow, because we don't know what it will bring. Today, this day, is all we have, so we should make the best of it.

At first, I was so literal-minded this made no sense to me. I would say, "That's just not possible. If I'm going to visit somebody, I have to let the people know I'm coming, I have to make the plane reservations. I don't understand this program."

Now I understand. Make plans, but don't project how those

72

plans will turn out. Live in the now, live this minute. You only *think* you can control what's going to happen. You may step off a curb and get hit by a car and never make your plane, so it's better to quit second-guessing God, and trust in Him.

That first year of recovery was confusing. I've said there was joy, I've said there was terror, I've said there was denial; sometimes I'd go through all of them in a few hours. I'm thinking of a day in New York. It was the first time I had come East since my treatment, and I was nervous. Jerry and I were still involved with the NBC contract, which we later bought ourselves out of, and we were staying at the Pierre. We were to give a dinner party there for Fred Silverman, who was the new president of NBC.

I was beside myself with anxiety, agitated in mind and body. I wanted desperately to take a tranquilizer because that was the only thing I knew that could help. Then I remembered Dr. Pursch telling us in lectures that tranquilizers have the same effect as a couple of dry martinis.

At that time, Jerry was still drinking martinis, and a pitcherful had been delivered to our room. There it was on the service cart, with a bucket of ice and a couple of glasses. It was a huge pitcher, and I knew if I took just a little bathroom glass and poured until it was about a third full, the liquor would never be missed. And I would be calm and cool and able to greet and entertain our important guests.

No one would ever know. But I would know. Honesty means self-honesty.

I didn't drink the martini. And the evening went beautifully. I realized I could do it without my old crutch. The growth of something like that is the growth of sobriety. Sobriety is progressive, the same way alcoholism is progressive. That one event has given me the strength to face many others.

There was other growth in our family. In September 1978, Gayle told us she was pregnant, and we rejoiced that we were going to have a grandchild. That same month—on September 14, I remember the date—I had my cosmetic surgery. We were just back from Vail, and I was feeling so good inside I decided I'd like to look just as good outside. The surgery caused a minor storm.

73

Some women who had admired me for my frankness about cancer and alcoholism pronounced themselves appalled by my vanity. This happened more on the East Coast than on the West, where people have their faces lifted as casually as they drink iced tea.

Three weeks later, the new face was unveiled—I was a centerfold in *People* magazine—and I went to a big bash honoring Fred Astaire in Los Angeles. Then Jerry and I celebrated our thirtieth wedding anniversary, and I accepted a humanitarian award in New Orleans, and there was a party at the Waldorf in New York to mark the coming out of *The Times of My Life*.

All this happened in less than two months. I can hear Meri Bell's voice in my ear: "You're doing too much, you're doing too much, you're doing too much. Please stop."

I didn't stop. And much of the time, I was having fun. I loved the book party at the Waldorf. Henry Kissinger spoke, and so did Pearl Bailey and Flip Wilson. Clara Powell came up from Washington. I wore a peach-colored chiffon dress, smiled at the press, noticed that a couple of people I knew were pretty tight, and thought, gee, that's too bad.

Which was a big step up from gee, I wish I had a brandy. Interviewers are always asking me if I'm ever tempted to take a pill or a drink. Sure, I've been tempted. I liked alcohol, it made me feel warm. And I loved pills, they took away my tension and my pain. So the thing I have to know is that I haven't got this problem licked; to the day I die, I'll be recovering.

From time to time, in these early days, there was publicity that hurt. Once I picked up a magazine that had an article on women and alcoholism, and there was a drawing of a woman completely disheveled, passed out on a couch, hair all over her face, clothes in disarray, beside a table with a bottle of liquor and pills spilled all around. And the first two words of the article were "Betty Ford." I closed the magazine and put it back, and I wondered if I'd been outspoken once too often, if maybe my alcoholism and recovery would have been better kept more quiet. All I could think was, so this is what they believe about me.

Thanksgiving of 1978 was eventful in many ways. Susan issued a bulletin. She said she and Chuck Vance were planning to be married. Jerry and I were not thrilled, and one of my greatest regrets is that we showed it. Susan was only twenty-one, Chuck a divorced man with adopted children, and while we said we would support their decision, we also said we thought they ought to wait a while. Susan was our youngest child, our only girl, and we didn't think anybody was good enough for her.

Once the romance became serious, Chuck had to be transferred from our Secret Service detail because it's frowned on for an agent to be dating the daughter of his protectee. He and Susan were angry about that, and when he was transferred to the Los Angeles field office, she went along with him. It was a case of, I'm twenty-one years old, and I'll do as I please. Then they came to us and said they wanted to be married. Well, I suppose we should have heaved a great sigh of relief, but we didn't have the sense.

Susan Ford Vance: "There was no fondness there, between my mother and Chuck. Even after we were married, she would say, 'Well, if things aren't going okay, honey, you can come home anytime.' And that really irritated me, that she had no confidence in my choice. I guess probably after about two years of my marriage, my parents finally gave in.

"The best thing they did—and we still laugh about this—was to go to Jordan right before the wedding, to visit King Hussein. And since Chuck and I moved the date up, we had only six weeks to plan everything, so Mother hired a social person who knew all the photographers in the desert, and where to get this and that, and then Mother took off for Jordan, and I planned the wedding with this gal. And Mother got back late enough so that anything I had planned she didn't like, she couldn't change.

"So instead of its being my mother's wedding, which is the way most daughters' weddings are, it was really mine. So many times, Chuck and I came close to running off to Las Vegas, saying, 'Let's just elope, and send them a telegram and tell 'em we got married, and forget it.' But we felt that just wouldn't be fair."

I did not want to go to Jordan. I was apprehensive. Not just about Susan's wedding. I was comfortable in my house, I didn't want to go out and test the waters. This would be a semi-official visit to the Middle East, and I wasn't ready for a lot of responsibility, I felt it was too soon.

Jerry put his foot down. "Make up your mind," he said. "You're going."

Jerry Ford: "It was not just a trip to Jordan, we were to visit Israel, Saudi Arabia, Egypt, and I insisted that Betty come. I felt it was good for our marriage to do things together. And during that early part of 1979, I would not have been comfortable going away without her for two weeks. I was concerned about leaving her home alone. Also, she had received a personal invitation from Crown Prince Fahd to come to Saudi Arabia, and I told her the State Department was anxious that she accept. Because for the Saudis to recognize a woman this way was a real breakthrough."

I was still taking orders then, I hadn't yet become assertive. So I abandoned my only daughter—that's the way it seemed to me—and went off on that much-dreaded trip, and had a perfectly fascinating time. History was being made, and one more time, I had a front-row seat. And one more time, it was totally by accident.

We went to Aswan with President Sadat of Egypt and his wife, Jihan. It was the night after the Shah and Shabanou of Iran had made their escape. We were unaware that they had fled till we met them at Aswan. President Sadat had had an entire hotel evacuated, and it was completely surrounded by soldiers. There was nobody there but the Shah and his wife, the Sadats, Jerry and me and all our staffs. We had dinner in this big empty room. There was a very deserted, spooky feeling to it.

The Shah was bitter, his wife despondent. I said something about skiing—she'd visited us in Vail—and she said, "Well, it will be a long time before I'll ski again."

In Jerusalem, Menachem Begin gave a dinner for us, and Jerry and I walked the streets Jesus had walked.

76

A break in the campaign swing—our rehearsal dinner. The candidate arrived for dessert!

The young congressional family in Washington, D.C., 1962.

Lady Bird Johnson welcomes me to the LBJ Library in Austin. Our backgrounds may put us on opposite sides of the political aisle, but we have shared a lot (like support of the ERA), 1976. [Photo by David Woo. Courtesy of Dallas Morning News]

Jerry was always proud of this label. [Cartoon by Rob Lawlor. Courtesy of the Philadelphia Daily News.]

A couple of experts on U.S. foreign policy discussing not ships, strategy or "Star Wars," but sushi, sashimi and tempura. (P.S., I'm not one of the experts!) [Photo courtesy of Kansai Television, Japan.]

A banquet at the Great Hall of the People in Beijing. Our conversation with Deng Xioping was animated and the food was more than ample. The trip added to our China experience and my waistline. March 1981.

The realization of a dream—groundbreaking for the Betty Ford Center, October 1981, with John Sinn, President of the Board of the Eisenhower Medical Center, left, and Leonard Firestone. [Photo courtesy of the Eisenhower Medical Center.]

This is the campus of the Betty Ford Center, which is located at the Eisenhower Medical Center. [Photo courtesy of the Eisenhower Medical Center.]

In Saudi Arabia, I sat at a sumptuous dinner table between Crown Prince Fahd and Oil Minister Sheik Yamani, who were not accustomed to breaking bread with an American woman visitor on a state occasion.

In Jordan, King Hussein and Queen Noor picked us up at the Amman airport, and he drove us away in his own car. He had two or three jeeps following behind him with machine guns. The next day, we boarded a big plane, which Hussein piloted, for a trip to his beachfront hideaway at Aqaba. Flying over the desert, we could look down and see Bedouins with their tents and camels, and an occasional fancy car. And when we got to the sea, King Hussein took us out on his yacht, and he steered that too.

We visited the ancient city of Petra, riding camels through a crease in the mountains. Someone brought a camel over to me and dared me to kiss it on the nose, and I did. I've often thought how lucky I was that the dumb thing didn't bite my chin off. The military had flown us to Petra (I had half expected King Hussein to do it, as he'd done everything else) in funny little bubble-nosed helicopters. You sit right up in the bubble, and feel as though you're out in space; those helicopters are like mosquitoes, buzzing up and down.

Across the centuries, Petra's sandstone bluffs have eroded into strange and marvelous shapes; from the east, you approach these ruins by way of a narrow gorge called the Sik.

Glorious, the whole experience I had wanted to avoid. I was still having sleeping problems, and I'd even worried that I wouldn't be able to sleep on the plane going over. As it turned out, none of the things I had feared came to pass. I went through the two weeks sober, clear-eyed and able to appreciate everything. And I thought about other times when my schedule had been heavy, and I had leaned on drugs and alcohol to keep me going, and later, could not remember half of what had happened.

One year earlier, I couldn't have made that trip, I had been too sick. Now I was physically well, I had some stamina, and I had been relieved of the obligation to keep up with whatever social drinking was being done by my companions. And I thought to myself, hey, I'm doing all right.

I had moments like that in recovery, when I was scared something terrible was going to happen because I felt too good.

We got home ten days before Susan's wedding. Everything was going swimmingly without me. The invitations were out, the designer, Estevez, had finished Susan's dress, arrangements had been made for the church, the orchestra, the caterer, the tent outside the house where the reception would be held.

Because Susan had panicked at the idea of a big wedding, she had switched from a large to a small church, but she hadn't sufficiently cut down the guest list, so not all the people who had been invited got into the small church. The day of the wedding, I spent a good deal of my time fretting about those left standing outside. Gayle, seven months pregnant, was matron of honor, and she spent a good deal of her time trying to get her bouquet to lie flat against her stomach.

The wedding and the few days right before the wedding are a jumble in my head. We were no sooner unpacked from our Middle Eastern trip than I raced over to Pasadena to help Pearl Bailey do a benefit. Then wedding guests started arriving from all over the country. We got through the rehearsal, and the rehearsal dinner, and the bridal breakfast, and the wedding itself at two-thirty in the afternoon, and the reception followed, replete with dancing and drinking and general merrymaking. Although my son Steve contends that I was not so merry as some of the others.

Steve Ford: "The reception was very hard for Mom. She couldn't stay in the tent the whole time, and I can remember going into the house and sitting with her. I'm sure she wanted to have a drink. You know, most of these guests were people she had not seen since the intervention, and this was a big day for her, a kind of coming out. It was a big deal, you know, your baby's getting married. I sat in the house with her and held her hand."

Susan Ford Vance: "She didn't even have a year of sobriety when we got married. The wedding, I think, was very hard on her. She told some friends of mine that until the moment I walked down the aisle, she never expected me to do it."

To some extent, I suppose both Steve and Susan are right, though I don't agree that I wanted to have a drink. Everything had been moving so fast, I was upset about losing our only daughter, and what I probably wanted was a few days of peace and quiet, which I couldn't schedule. I had board meetings at Eisenhower, there were lunches and parties and a lot of television shots because there was interest in my book, and I was required by contract to make appearances and do the talk shows.

And maybe it *was* all too much too soon. Because in the spring of 1979, I fell into a depression I couldn't shake off in one day or two or three. A while back, I discovered evidence of this in an old notebook.

"I seem to be in a cycle of negative thinking," I had written. "Why? My health is good, summer is coming, we will get away to Vail, I'm a brand-new grandmother [Sarah Joyce Ford had been born in April], what more can I ask?

"Have I been thinking about myself too much, and not enough about those less fortunate? Has playing the martyr become old hat? Am I looking for more worlds to conquer, and not finding any? Have people built me up too much? I am so far from being perfect, from perfecting myself, and it always surprised me when I was perceived as a heroine. Still, I have enjoyed helping others; maybe I need a new cause, a new challenge."

Then, on my sixty-first birthday, a new challenge came my way. Though I did not instantly recognize it. It began with a phone call from Nicky Firestone to tell me that she and Leonard would not be coming to our house for dinner. "Leonard's in terrible shape," she said.

6

Even in our sleep, pain which cannot
forget falls drop by drop upon the heart
until in our despair, against our will,
comes wisdom through the awful grace
of God.

Aeschylus

Leonard Firestone: "I think all alcoholics have a tendency to be suicidal. I used to wake up in the morning and feel so lousy, and I'd get up, go get a couple of drinks, get back in bed and know I'd pass out soon. And I'd think, oh, if I only wouldn't wake up again, this whole damn thing would be over. I didn't have the guts to do anything to myself, but I wished I would die."

Pat Benedict was staying with us that weekend. She had come to help celebrate not only my birthday but the first anniversary of my sobriety. When Nicky called, I said, "Why don't you talk to Pat?" Nicky was reluctant. "I hate to bother her," she said, "she's just down here for a couple of days' vacation."

Nicky Firestone: "I said I didn't want to bother Pat. 'That would be a busman's holiday,' I said. 'She's here for fun and your birthday party, she doesn't want to be mixed up in this thing, he's a mess, and I can't impose on her.' 'Well,' Betty said, 'she'd love to see Leonard.' "

Pat Benedict: "Ordinarily, I don't hang out in Palm Springs. I work at a juvenile hall with street kids. But I was down there for Betty's birthday, and I was in the Fords' pool, when Betty came to the edge. 'I hate to ask you,' she said, 'because you're supposed to be down here resting, but Mr. Firestone's in trouble.' And I said, 'So?'

"I had only met Leonard once. That was when I was taking care of Betty. Steve and I had been out walking, and we met him, and Steve commented to me. He said, 'I think Mr. Firestone's been drinking.' And I said, 'Steve, he's not only been drinking, he's drunk.' Leonard and I laugh about that now."

Nicky Firestone: "The first time I met Leonard, he was drunk. That was back in 1965. It was at a party, and he had a glass in his hand, and I asked him, 'What's that?' and he said, 'Vodka. And don't give me any of that God stuff.' (The friends who introduced us had told him I was a Christian Scientist.) I told him the vodka wasn't going to do him a bit of good, and walked away. Shortly after that, he went to Menninger's, and he was there two weeks and he came back to Los Angeles, and started going to meetings. After we married, he was sober for a long time."

Leonard Firestone: "In 1965, I woke up in a hospital and my three kids were standing at the foot of the bed, and they said, 'You have to do something.' 'Okay,' I said, 'I'll go to Los Angeles and join AA.' They said no, I'd tried that once and it hadn't worked. And finally, my daughter said, 'Will you do something you don't want to do? Just for us?'

"Well, you know, I was so beat and hung over, and you have to be a real low-down not to respond to three loving kids when they're so concerned, so I said yes, I'd do whatever they wanted me to. They said they wanted me to go to Menninger's, they had a company plane outside, and in ten minutes, I was on my way to Topeka, Kansas.

"In those days, there was great secrecy surrounding the subject of alcoholism. My secretary said to my son, 'I'm very careful not to tell anybody where your father is,' and Brooks said, 'I don't think Dad would care, there's no shame in doing something about your problem, the shame is in not doing something.' That was profound, but at the time, I don't think it made much impression on me. I was a little frightened, I just had the feeling I didn't want everybody to know I was going in for treatment.

"After I came back from Menninger's, I went nine years without a drink, and then I thought I had it under control, that I'd built up a tolerance. So I started again with a little sherry, and then some martinis. For about eight or nine months, I got away with it. Then one night, boom! Down the drain I went. For a couple of years.

"The point—and I try to make this point to patients when I lecture at the Betty Ford Center—is that an alcoholic is never cured. There is no way an alcoholic can build up a tolerance that will permit him to drink. I found this out the hard way."

There's a story Leonard tells in his lectures. It's about the driver of a sixteen-wheeler truck who has to take an oral test before the state will renew his license. "You're coming down a steep grade in the truck," the examiner says. "What would you do?"

"I'd just keep going straight ahead," the driver says.

"You're carrying a load of dynamite," the examiner says. "What would you do?"

"Just keep going straight ahead," the driver says.

"You're almost to a railroad crossing, and you look down a hill and see a slow freight going across the tracks at the bottom of the hill. What would you do?"

"Jam on my brakes."

"You don't have any brakes. What would you do?"

"I'd wake up Ambrose, who is sleeping in the cab next to me."

"Why would you wake up Ambrose?"

83

"Well," says the driver, "Ambrose is just a country boy, and he's never seen the kind of wreck we're gonna have."

That was the kind of wreck Leonard was headed for, in April 1979, a scant year after I'd had my own crash. He was very dear to Jerry and me, but it was up to Nicky and his family to take action, and Nicky was reluctant.

Nicky Firestone: "Back then, I didn't realize what intervention meant. Betty had talked, but it's like sharing someone else's experiences that you don't really understand. Still, when she urged me to go speak to Pat, I did. And the next thing I knew, Pat was saying, 'Could I see Mr. Firestone?' I said, 'Surely, but he's in terrible condition.'

"We walked across the lawn and into the guest room. I had Leonard out in the guest room, and I'd put the liquor there too. With an alcoholic, it doesn't do any good to take it away, they'll find it, and I didn't want him marching around looking for it, and falling into the pool.

"Pat talked to him, and she came out and said, 'You'll have to do something, he's in very serious condition. I don't know what his blood pressure is because I don't have my tools, but I can guarantee it's abnormally high.'

"Through Joe Cruse, we got a doctor who came immediately, and the minute he walked in, Leonard dismissed him. In a very imperious manner. He said his good friend Pat Benedict—whom he had just met, by the way—would take care of him."

Pat Benedict: "When Nicky came over to talk to me, for some reason I remember she was wearing a pair of white slacks and a blue shirt and a white hat. She was panicky. I said, 'I'd be happy to go see him, but that's all.' She said, 'What do you mean?' I said, 'My talking to him won't work if you need an intervention.' I went across to the house with her and she took me in and said to Leonard, 'You remember Pat,' and he said, 'Oh, my old friend Pat.' Hell, he didn't remember me from nuthin'. The doctor arrived, and said Leonard's blood pressure was way up 'and we're going to put you in Eisenhower.' 'Oh, no,' Leonard said, 'my old friend Pat will take care of me.' And I thought, God, here we go again.

"I stayed with Leonard in the guest room. That evening, I went over to eat Betty's birthday dinner, and when I went back, Nicky was out on the patio. I said, 'How's Mr. Firestone?' and she said, 'Why, he's sleeping,' and I said, 'No, he isn't. Look, he's over there in the icebox, getting a drink.' Nicky hadn't even heard him.

"Nicky hired a night nurse. Leonard fired her. He said, 'Pat will take care of me.'

Nicky Firestone: "His 'good friend Pat Benedict' did take care of him, and the doctor started him on medication, and we took the liquor away. Len was beginning to be detoxed, and the next thing I knew, Betty had got hold of Joe Pursch, the intervention had been set up, and I felt I'd been railroaded. I didn't have time to think. I said, 'I can't take full responsibility for this.' We were dealing with someone else's life. And he was an adult. True, he was in bad shape, but he was perfectly competent to make a decision.

"Finally, I phoned Leonard's son, Brooks, and I gave him Dr. Pursch's number. I said, 'You call him and talk to him and you make the decision. I feel your father has to have help, but I want us all to be in accord.'

"Brooks came down—his father didn't know he was here—and the next day, we had this surprise intervention."

Pat Benedict: "The next morning, I got Leonard dressed, and I was sitting on the divan rubbing his feet, and in walked President Ford and Betty and Nicky and Brooks and Joe Pursch. And Leonard looked at them and he looked at me and he looked at them and he looked back at me and he said, 'I think I know what's coming.' "

Leonard Firestone: "When they all came in, I was lying on the couch, I was being detoxed, and Pat began to rub my feet. I loved that, I thought she was doing it to be nice. She was doing it to hold me on the couch so I couldn't go and get a drink, and I'd be there when the intervention came.

"In the old days, they thought you had to get in the gutter before you could get help. Well, I was in a mental gutter. I'd never be in a literal gutter. I have too much money and too many friends, and they could take care of me and find me doctors and hospitals. But the mental gutter is just as bad, and when your friends and family point this out to you, you've got to accept it, and say, 'What do you want me to do?' "

Nicky Firestone: "Basically, Leonard knew he was alcoholic, because he'd had other treatment. But he tried to wiggle out of it. He knew the minute we walked in what was going on, because Betty had had her intervention the year before. And as he wiggled, the doors closed, one after another. None of them gave. It's terribly emotional because you speak very honestly, you say what you feel, what you as a person can put up with and what you can't put up with.

"Intervention is tough because it's relentless, but it's kind. You don't scream at each other, but you don't give up, you keep hammering until the alcoholic gives in.

"It's the most wonderful concept. Every alcoholic used to kind of feel he or she was the only one. A friend of mine said she thought she was the only person on Park Avenue that had a drinking problem, and she was so ashamed of it she used to hide her bottles in her bedroom and then take them down to the bottom of the apartment house and put them in the garbage because she didn't want them on her floor. Now there are just miraculous things for people to do, places for them to go. The knowledge you get, the knowledge that other people have the same problem, it's all coming together."

Pat Benedict: "When Leonard said he would be willing to go to AA, Betty said, 'No, no, no, Leonard, you're going to go to treatment.'

"The President and Betty were great, you would have thought they did this every day. President Ford said, 'You're my best friend, Leonard, and I'm not going to let you lie over here and die.'

"Leonard's son Brooks did a beautiful job too."

Dr. Pursch: "Leonard was not delighted to have this thing sprung on him, and he was obviously bowled over by the President and Mrs. Ford's being there. He wondered how it all happened; he wondered, when he saw me, 'Who is this guy?' After it was set that he would go for treatment, I said, 'You have just made the right choice,' and he said, 'You know, I don't really like you. You act like you've got the only way.' And I said, 'No, no, only the best way.'"

Dr. Pursch says the reason Leonard's intervention didn't take long was that by then we were all experts. It did work pretty well, and Leonard and Nicky got bundled up into the car and went on over to an alcoholic rehab that Dr. Pursch (who had by then retired from the Navy) was running.

Leonard Firestone: "I didn't like Joe Pursch at first, but after treatment, I realized he was one of the best friends I ever had for what he did for me. When I went to treatment—it was my second go after nine years of sobriety—I was very ashamed that I fell down again. I went there and got detoxed, and when I had to call friends, and cancel some business appointments, and a golf match, I told everyone, 'I'm down here at a rehab,' and if they said, 'What's that?' I'd say, 'Well, I'm doing the same thing Betty Ford did.' It was a crutch, you know? I wouldn't do that today. I'm not proud of the fact that I'm an alcoholic, but I'm not ashamed of it. I mean, I have the disease, and that's it. Betty took a lot of the stigma out of it."

Nicky Firestone: "When Leonard came out, he and Betty got together with Joe Cruse, who had done a lot of the groundwork, and they began working on plans for a place that eventually became the Betty Ford Center."

At Long Beach, there was no idea in the back of my mind that I was going to go home and start a treatment center, any more than there had been an idea in my mind as a young girl that I was going to go out and be an alcoholic.

That first year of my sobriety, I just wanted to get my own life turned around. But always there was the mail. "I need help." "Please help." "How did you do it?" "Tell me the formula."

I wasn't ready to get involved. And then came the weekend of my birthday and Leonard's intervention, and I *could* offer help to another person who was a dear friend and a good neighbor.

And it worked. Leonard found his recovery, as I found mine, and together, we started out to try and give something back.

7

Thanks be to God, since my leaving
drinking of wine, I do find myself much
better, and do mind my business better,
and do spend less money, and less time
lost in idle company.

Samuel Pepys

In the next three years, Leonard and I probably did lose less time
in idle company, and spend less money; we were out *collecting*
money to start an alcohol and drug rehabilitation center; friends
saw us coming with our hands out and sighed deeply.

Let me say a little more about Leonard here. To put it simply, he's a great man. Once he retired from the big industrialist
game, he went into public service. He served as our Ambassador
to Belgium; now he labors not only for the Betty Ford Center but
for other rehabs in the desert—Turnoff (the place Joe Cruse had
Susan take pictures of), which is for kids, and Lost Heads, which is
a place where people with limited funds can go.

The only thing that can deter Leonard even briefly from
good works is a golf game—he's been described as a gentleman
hustler—and for all that he's hung out with crowned heads, he is
plainspoken, unpretentious, funny and, most of all, dear.

I'm thinking back to April of 1978, and the dinner party I
hadn't wanted to attend at the Firestones', the one Pursch in-

sisted I get over there for, right before I went into treatment. Leonard had told Nicky he wanted to buy me flowers. "I want to get her an orchid wrist corsage."

"Ladies don't wear wrist corsages anymore," Nicky said. Leonard was adamant. "I don't care whether they do or not. That's what I want to get her."

A year later, we packed *him* off for treatment, and when he came back, there was something different about him. The change was so apparent to his friends that Walter Annenberg cross-examined him. Leonard seemed to have an inner peace, and Walter wanted to know where it came from, what Leonard had done to get it. "What did they give you in treatment? What is it that you have found?"

Leonard, who is never pompous, even about weighty subjects, said, "I found I was allergic to alcohol. You might say I've got a busted filter. I used to be able to drink but I can't drink anymore, so I've learned to let go. And I've learned I needed love and understanding and help from counseling and a Higher Power."

After that exchange, Leonard called me up in great excitement. Walter (who is trustee emeritus of the Eisenhower Medical Center) had suggested that Leonard and I put our heads together and come up with a plan for starting an alcoholic treatment center at Eisenhower.

Well, I had already been trying to help Joe Cruse get a treatment center started in the area. Once we went to see an old ranch he thought had possibilities. The White Sun Guest Ranch and Country Club was a place where people used to come to honeymoon, it had been there a long time, and Joe believed it could be developed into a facility like Hazelden. He had also attempted to convince the board at Eisenhower Medical Center that Eisenhower should include a rehab facility. He didn't have much luck.

The feeling Joe got was that the board wasn't ready. I don't know. But I do know that with my recovery, and Leonard's recovery, and Walter Annenberg's awed response to Leonard's serenity, everything changed.

At this point President John Sinn suggested to the rest of the board, "Let's take a look at whether or not this idea of Betty's and Leonard's is a good and logical one."

They took a look. And confirmed our opinion; the Coachella Valley had more than its share of drinkers. More treatment centers for alcoholism were needed in the community. There was only one, although records showed that many of the county's automobile accidents were alcohol- and drug-related.

It used to be that alcoholics were given four or five days' treatment in an acute-care facility, and then released. The alcoholic would leave, stay sober for maybe thirty days, then start drinking again. It was a revolving door. Sometimes they couldn't even get admitted to a hospital unless they had a stomach problem, or a chest problem, some illness the hospital felt competent to deal with.

Dolores Hope: "I was excited that this issue was going to be addressed, that somebody was going to do something about it. We were having a problem at Eisenhower because we were getting alcoholic patients, and under the provisions of an acute-care hospital, we weren't really supposed to take them in. We were getting criticism from Medicare and other insurance outfits about giving alcoholics beds. Betty, God bless her, told the board alcoholism was a disease, and it had to be treated as you would treat any other disease. But not necessarily in an acute-care hospital."

Well, we—John Sinn, Leonard and I—went out to see if we could raise funds for this thing, and in the beginning, our biggest contributors were the McCallum Foundation and Leonard himself. Each gave half a million dollars. And I had some good luck, though not the usual kind, in Las Vegas. Walter Probst, who's on the Eisenhower board, flew a bunch of us over for a Sammy Davis opening, and there was a big dinner, and gambling, and then the show, and everybody was drinking wine, and having a good time, and all of a sudden somebody said to somebody else, "You mean you haven't given any cash to Betty's project?" and they started pledging, and by the time it was over, I had people signed up to the tune of a quarter of a million dollars.

Most of these donors were on the Eisenhower board, and I was encouraged because I felt that meant we really had their blessing.

We decided that anybody who gave half a million dollars could have his or her name on a building, and discovered we had some friends who didn't want their names on buildings, they wrote the checks and let the credit go.

Leonard and I got a lesson from the CEO of a large oil company when we went to him for money. "How much do you want?" he said. "Fifty thousand dollars," we said. We were on a private plane, flying back from a golfing weekend in Augusta, Georgia, and we were the CEO's guests, so we felt a little sheepish about hitting him up for a donation, even in a good cause. He shook his head at our ineptitude. "Don't ever go in asking for what you want," he said. "Ask for twice as much, and maybe you'll get it." Then he gave us a hundred thousand dollars.

We traveled around. We went up to Hazelden, one of the oldest and best-known rehab centers in the country, and took bookkeepers with us to look over how they kept their records; since Joe and Leonard and I had all been to different treatment centers, we borrowed freely from every one of them. We invited experts onto our task force. Ed Johnsen, a builder and developer, came in with us and helped us more than I can tell.

Ed Johnsen: "They have a tendency, in 'society' projects, to have a lot of committees that meet. Sometimes you need a few people on those committees who say, 'Let's do something, not just meet and schedule another meeting.'

"Having put up many homes and commercial buildings, I was able to help a little on the plot plans. Dolores and the top level of trustees at Eisenhower had offered us a portion of the Eisenhower campus; we had the choice of the northeast corner or the southeast corner, and we picked the southeast. It was close to eight acres. We drew up the schematics, the land layout was accepted, the concept was accepted, and a very good commercial architect went to work on the first buildings. They were a bit blockish for my taste, so we put some trees on a couple of the blank walls."

We got our money relatively quickly. We had three million dollars by the third anniversary of my sobriety. And all this time, we were also working on getting legislation passed so we could go ahead and build.

We contended that we could maintain quality recovery at about a third the cost of what was being charged in acute-care hospitals, but there was no licensing in the state of California for the type of bed we were proposing. We had to convince the state, which meant getting a bill introduced in the legislature. Fortunately, I had a friend who was well connected.

Jerry Ford: "I contacted Governor Brown and members of the state legislature. We got hold of a key senator who was in a position to help, and it was his parliamentary skill, along with later help from a member of the California assembly, that got the bill through. The Senator managed to have it added as a rider to some other piece of legislation, and then I called Jerry Brown to make sure he didn't veto it.

"The sequel is that a year later, after the Center was built and operating, this senator was running for reelection, and he called in his chips. He asked Betty and me to come up and participate in a fund-raising event, and we had no choice. We were indebted to him."

The bill went through in thirty days, but that was only the beginning. Then a committee had to prepare the regulations. For a year, we went back and forth, to and from Sacramento, and met with other people who were running treatment centers, and with state officials, and with doctors working for the state. One of the big arguments was whether to have nurses around the clock. We said we didn't want that.

Nicky Firestone: "They had to go through this legislation because the center was to be a freestanding unit—that is, it wasn't physically connected to a hospital. It would still have all the medical protection of a hospital, but not the expenses, because they didn't need, for instance, to have oxygen in every room. Or trained nurses around the clock. They could get oxygen and emergency care in the flick of an eye, at Eisenhower Hospital. Quicker than you could in a lot of big city hospitals. You could go across the grounds from the Betty Ford Center and be in emergency in two minutes.

"Leonard and Betty worked for months and months with committee members, haggling over details. Deciding whether the proper word in a given phrase should be 'to,' 'for,' 'if,' 'it' or 'but.'

"Then they got it put together, and they hired the staff—Joe Cruse was in charge of that—and all of a sudden, there it was. A miracle. Of course they had loads of help, but it was a miracle anyway."

We were to be on probation for a year, because we were a pilot project. If it hadn't worked, if we hadn't done what we said we were going to do, if we hadn't proven ourselves, they would not have given us a license. When the year was up, we had our license and we were accredited. We had established a type of care, a type of bed, that the state—and insurance companies—found acceptable.

Sometimes, as we struggled through those endless sessions in Sacramento, I was so grateful for John Sinn, who was our anchor. As a hospital president, he had such vast experience in the ways of government bureaucracy, and hospital administration. All hospitals are run by books of regulations; there's a regulation about how they take out the trash, there's a regulation about how they dispense medication—Leonard got bored with the procedure. He just wanted it to be over and done. "We've put it together," he said. "We know we can provide quality care in a non-institutional setting at a low cost. What's the problem?" It was the cry of a man who'd successfully run a big business banging his head against a bureaucracy. But we made it.

Somewhere in the middle of the process, Leonard, Joe Cruse and John Sinn asked if they could call the new facility the Betty Ford Center. I said I was honored, but I didn't think so. "What are you trying to do," I said, "paint me into a corner? I'll never be able to drink again!" They convinced me that it would be beneficial to our cause if I allowed my name to be used. It was definitely not my desire. What's more, they made me president of the board. I love the work, and it gives me a chance to lord it over my husband. I say, "Honey, you're just a former president, I am an acting president."

It was a hectic sobriety I was going through while the Center was being built. I was a recovering alcoholic who wanted to have a say in every decision, to have her finger in every pie. My perfectionist spirit coming to the fore again.

When Leonard and I were not on the road drumming up funds, I was traveling with Jerry. We went around the world—to Paris, Tokyo, half a dozen other places. We went to Grand Rapids for the dedication of the Gerald R. Ford Museum. We went to Detroit for the 1980 Republican convention.

In Detroit, I said a lot of prayers. Along the lines of "God, it's in Your hands." Because it looked as though Jerry might be talked into running with Reagan. I knew I shouldn't try to force on him my feelings of not wanting to go back to Washington, of wanting to stay in the desert. I thought of leaving behind the Betty Ford Center, with our work so newly started, and the familiarity of my support groups, and I turned it over. I absolutely let go. I kept repeating, "Thy will, not my will," all the while hoping He might see fit to exercise His will in an agreeable direction.

Jerry Ford: "In 1979, there had been a lot of support for my going after the Republican presidential nomination. I looked at the pluses and minuses—I could lose the nomination, and even if I won the nomination, I might not be elected—and it just made more sense not to get into it. It would have been a replay of the 1976 confrontation between Reagan and me, bitter, counterproductive, and in the end, would have jeopardized the possibility of a Republican victory in November.

"In June of 1980, after I had made the announcement to the press that I would not run for the nomination, President Reagan called and said he'd like to come talk to me, and we met in my office, and he said he hoped I would consider being on the ticket with him. I said I didn't want to be Vice President. 'I can do more good for you by campaigning,' I said, 'and I will.'

"I thought the matter was settled. Then Betty and I flew to Detroit, and the day after we arrived there, President Reagan again asked if he could see me. And when he came over—it was right at the time of my birthday—he brought a peace pipe as a present. Again, he said they wanted me to be on the ticket. I said, in deference to his request, I would reconsider. We selected four people—Henry Kissinger, Alan Greenspan, Bob Barrett and Jack Marsh, all of whom had been in the Ford White House—to meet with four from the Reagan staff, and they tried to put into writing what my responsibilities as Vice President would be.

"After about thirty-six hours, it became obvious that it was impossible, and I said to President Reagan, 'I think we ought not to try to do this.'

"Betty's recovery was never talked about, but if I had run— for President or Vice President—and in the process it had interfered with her recovery, I would never have forgiven myself. So even though it was not discussed, subjectively it was a factor."

I was more than grateful for the way it played out. I was relieved. My new life in recovery was precious to me and I was glad to be done with politics. I had eaten enough creamed chicken and sat through enough speeches to have earned a presidential pardon. At one time during my husband's administration I made the smart-aleck remark that a First Lady ought to be paid, she had a full-time job, and I'm not sure I wasn't right.

When your husband is serving, you're an extension of him, you can't always express the way you feel, and I'd never been good at keeping my mouth shut if I had a strong opinion. In the White House, I had embraced the Equal Rights Amendment, I had said I'd been to a psychiatrist, many of my public statements might have mortified a lesser man than Jerry.

Even in Detroit, I was still having to be careful. I had come to Michigan knowing that there was going to be a march for ERA—I had packed a white dress, because the marchers had been asked to wear white—and I wanted to be a part of it.

I can't tell you how many Republicans came to try and talk me out of it. They said it wouldn't reflect well on the party if I marched. I was mad at the party anyway. The Republicans had been first to support ERA, and now they were dropping the ERA plank from their platform. But finally Jerry himself asked me not to go. "As a favor to me," he put it. He didn't *tell* me not to, because the minute anybody tells me I can't do something, I have to prove I can. Though I'm getting better, the longer I'm sober.

So I didn't march. I stood there in the window of our hotel suite, and watched the parade go by, a dutiful wife and a disappointed feminist in one quivering package.

Other days, there were other wonders outside that window.

Ann Cullen: "The Renaissance Center Hotel is three great glass towers. It's so big you need bread crumbs to find your way around it. While we were there, a wild storm came up, and the management called us from downstairs and said to pull the blinds shut so that if the windows broke, they wouldn't cut anyone, and then to go hug an interior wall.

"I plastered myself against an interior wall, and looked around for Mrs. Ford, and she was pressed flat against a window, peering out."

Well, I'm a fatalist. And it was a wonderful storm, a wonderful freak of nature, and I wanted to look around and see how far it went. I wouldn't have missed it for the world.

Ann Cullen: "She is a fatalist. During 1980, there were not only dozens of task force meetings about the Center, but there was also a full swing of speaking events for Mrs. Ford, and on one plane—it was a small jet—going from Westchester to Florida, we flew through another terrible thunderstorm. The President was with us, he was on his way to talk in Boca Raton, and Mrs. Ford was going to give a speech in Fort Lauderdale for the ERA. The lightning was everywhere, you couldn't get under it, you couldn't get over it, sandwiches were flying all around the cabin, at one moment a bolt of lightning flashed right through the plane. And President and Mrs. Ford were sitting quietly, holding hands, and she said to him, 'Well, honey, maybe this is it.' And I said, 'Great, but did you have to take me with you?' "

It does go through your mind: I wonder if this is going to be the last flight I ever take. Once when I was young, like Ann, and it would have been more serious—we had four little kids at home— we flew out of Aspen in a blinding snowstorm. This was an exception for us, since we usually went on separate flights. We were heading right into the mountains, and you couldn't even see the tips of the plane's wings, it was like being in a bullet. Nobody said a word, we all just watched the altimeter and willed the plane to for God's sake get up, get over those mountains.

You have to have a sense of humor at moments like that. There's an end to everybody's life, and there is not much we can do about it. It's no use to say, 'Stop! I'm not ready.'

Terrible things happen. I was standing in my kitchen when my husband called and told me President Kennedy had been killed. We were in Tokyo when we got word that President Reagan had been shot. When Jerry was President, two different lunatics tried to murder him. Qaddafi has threatened that he has terrorists right here in the United States. But I don't waste time worrying about the possibility of disaster. A golf ball could come over my roof and hit me on the head while I was out picking roses. I believe when your time is up, your time is up, and you will proceed to the promised land. You hope.

Jerry feels the same way. He is incredibly matter-of-fact in the face of danger. When he was shot at in Sacramento, he was en route to pay a courtesy call on Governor Brown. After the incident, he just continued on his way, walked into Brown's office and never uttered a word about what had happened. "Why should I?" he says.

In Detroit, in 1980, there were events to which I wasn't invited, and I survived. I went ahead and made other plans. The reason I tell this is that I feel it demonstrates a measure of recovery. Once, I might have been humiliated at not being on certain guest lists, but I had already built enough self-confidence so I could face the fact that I wasn't a favorite of everyone's. And that was all right. Not everybody is a favorite of mine.

You get well gradually. It doesn't happen overnight. It's like Muriel Zink said, "Treatment is really just your major detox, it gives you some tools to work with."

It isn't that I never get angry anymore, it's just that I try not to be consumed by my anger. Alcoholics don't handle anger well, but you learn in your program that you can't allow yourself to wallow in it.

And once again, I was realizing how much more fun it is to travel when you're straight. I was seeing, hearing, tasting with a sharpness I thought I'd lost. Sometimes, what I tasted was unexpected, as in Tokyo. It was in 1981 that Nancy Kissinger and I traveled to Tokyo with our husbands for what Jerry describes as "a thoughtful discussion on foreign policy."

Among the events for which the two men had promised to show up was a television talk show. To analyze matters of state, they assumed. But when we got to the studio—Nancy and I went along—the hosts said, "We want you to come sit down, and we are going to serve you Japanese food."

All four of us were ushered in, seated and offered various Japanese delicacies, and then we were requested to say what we thought of them. It was very hard on Henry's ego. One of the great minds of the Western world, and instead of asking his opinion about world affairs, the interviewers wanted to know what he thought of raw fish.

There was another trip—an around-the-world jaunt on which Leonard and Nicky also went. We were in Chungking, China, when someone in our group said, "We haven't had any rice yet. Why not?" and our guide said, "Rice is for working people and tourists, not for banquets. If they do serve rice at a banquet, it comes at the end, and the protocol is to say, 'Oh, no, thank you, I've had quite enough.' It's an insult if you take rice after they have given you their finest cuisine."

Well, Nicky hadn't heard this conversation. And that night, at the end of dinner with the mayor of Chungking and all the top brass, they brought out the rice. And I said, "Oh, no, thank you, I've had quite enough." And the next thing I heard was Nicky saying, "Oh, rice, I just love rice, and I haven't had any on this whole trip." And she started filling her plate, and it was hard for me not to burst out laughing. She had no idea she had just broken all tradition.

We went for a wonderful boat trip on the Yangtze River, and just to stir things up, the Secret Service agents told us there would be nine hundred people on board, and only four bathrooms. This so alarmed Nicky that she ran out and bought a little cooking pot with a handle on it. She was going to be prepared. Well, it turned out that our comparatively small party was assigned one entire enormous deck of the boat, and there were plenty of very adequate bathrooms. When we disembarked, Nicky left her cooking pot behind. Or tried to.

She had no sooner started down the gangplank than a Chinese steward came chasing after her crying, "Missy Firestone! Missy Firestone! You forget pot!" She couldn't lose that thing.

When Jerry was President, and we went to China in 1975, it was very cold. Packing for the trip home, reporters would try to leave torn panty hose in the wastebaskets, or long underwear, because they didn't need it anymore. Television people buy long underwear for a trip, charge it to their networks, and then, rather than wash it, abandon it. But you can't abandon goods in China. The Chinese had been so poor they didn't understand how anyone would throw anything away, and furthermore, they were so honest, they just packed up the panty hose and long underwear and mailed them to their owners at the next port of call. So there was no way "Missy" Firestone was going to leave behind a brand-new, unused pot!

We had good times, the Firestones and the Fords. We'd had

100

good times in our drinking days, and we had good times in our days of sobriety.

In Paris, I procured my first and only Chanel suit.

In Jakarta, I fed gorgeous tropical birds and never realized until later that what I had been plunging my hand into was a bowl of fat white grubs.

People drank all around us; it didn't bother Leonard or me. One of the things we'd both learned in treatment was, it was our choice to drink or not to drink. Although sometimes somebody chooses for you, and you find yourself surprised. I remember that one time at a dinner party in a restaurant—we were guests, so were the Firestones—an ice was served, after a fish course.

Everybody started eating, and once I'd had a couple of spoonfuls, I realized it was champagne, straight champagne, frozen, and then mushed up.

I sat there, spoon raised, thinking, this is absolutely divine, and I looked across the table to where Len was sitting, and he had his spoon raised too. Now it was early in his sobriety, it was his first year, and our eyes met, and we both smiled, said, "Um-hmm," and put our spoons down.

For a recovering person, it's very dangerous to take that first bite, sip, slug of anything alcoholic. Abstinence is the only guarantee of sobriety. Besides, for some people, one drink is all it takes. They wake up a week or two later, after a total binge, and they never again come back to a support group.

Even if you're an "episodic" alcoholic, that first drink is dangerous for what it does to your head. You start thinking, gee, I didn't fall down or turn green, maybe everybody got too excited about my being sick, maybe I wasn't so sick. If you should be unlucky enough not to get drunk with the first drink, the next week you're saying, well, that glass of wine last week didn't affect me, so I think I'll have another one. And when the second one doesn't affect you either, it's too late, you're on your way.

That's why they say it's not the tenth drink or the twelfth drink or the hundredth drink, it's the first drink you have to watch out for, it's the first drink that causes the turnaround and

101

begins to undermine the truth. Which is that alcoholics cannot drink, ever, if they expect to stay well.

On September 18, 1981, a little more than a year before the Betty Ford Center was dedicated, we dedicated the Gerald R. Ford Museum. Only a man as well liked as my husband could have pulled such a crowd to Grand Rapids. The Reagans came, and the Bushes, and the President of France, and the Foreign Minister of Japan and the Prime Minister of Canada and the President of Mexico and Lady Bird Johnson and Teddy Kennedy and Tip O'Neill and Bob Dole and Margaret Truman.

Bob Hope did a television special from Grand Rapids—I was his partner in a brief soft-shoe number—and the whole University of Michigan Marching Band performed, and there were banquets at night and parades in the daytime. The festivities were many and colorful.

I rode a float, and the weather was freezing, and the crowds were so large it took mounted police to control them, which is pretty unusual for Grand Rapids. In fact, my agents and I were caught out in the middle of the mob when I was supposed to be at the Museum with my husband, greeting the Reagans. We couldn't get through. *C'est la guerre.*

The networks came and did television for two days, and there was so much security in the hotel with all these heads of state that you couldn't get up or down in an elevator.

The Museum turned out to be absolutely splendid. Built on a riverbank, in the middle of a huge clear park, it's filled with memorabilia gathered from the State Department. And from me. I went through many old trunks looking for Jerry's baby shoes and baby clothes. His mother had saved his Boy Scout uniforms, and his Navy uniforms, and that's one of the nicest things about his museum. It's not a monument to greatness, it's a monument to the average man. It's a museum in the town where Jerry grew up, the town that knew him as a schoolboy, as a football player, as a son of the middle class who grew up to be President. It sort of says, this can happen to anyone.

One of the most beautiful things in it is a complete full-scale reproduction of the Oval Office in the White House. It's perfect in every detail, down to the acanthus leaves carved into the door moldings, with the draperies, the appointments, the furniture reproduced as they were when Jerry was President, clock, books, family photographs in place.

People come in there, and they suddenly fall quiet. It's unbelievable, like being in the real Oval Office.

There were many trips in 1980, '81, '82. Some were for pleasure, some were for duty, most were to raise money for the Betty Ford Center. Always, there was the ongoing business of the Center. I wanted to be involved in everything. I helped choose the chairs, the carpeting, the pictures on the walls, the colors of the bedspreads. I also helped to hire personnel.

John Schwarzlose: "I first met Betty in February of 1982. I was a consultant to the Hazelden Foundation in Minnesota (I was also running a program for alcoholics back in Peoria, Illinois) and the people at Hazelden had recommended me to Joe Cruse. Joe was medical director of the BFC, and they were looking for a program director. This was before the center was open.

"When Betty interviewed me, we discussed my feelings concerning treatment but in particular how I would assimilate the AA program and ideals into the BFC treatment program. I could see her wondering if I, as a non-alcoholic, would be able to run such a program.

"She asked me other questions too. 'What is important to you?' 'What are your outside interests?'

"A month later, I got a phone call offering me the job.

"I already had over ten years in the field. My experience dated back to 1972. While finishing up a master's degree in psychology, I'd had to spend some time at a state hospital in Illinois, and one of the units they put me on was the alcoholic unit. Then I spent a couple of terms on a mental health unit. The contrast was startling. On the alcoholic unit, there was a positiveness, you could see the men and women getting well. So I got very excited, but at that time, professionals with academic degrees didn't want to have anything to do with alcoholism. One of my professors said, 'John, you have such a bright future, don't waste your life with a bunch of drunks.'

"To this day, that is not an unusual point of view. A doctor recently visited the Betty Ford Center and he told us that in his city 90 percent of the alcoholic and drug treatment beds are in psychiatric hospitals. That's where the authorities believe they should be, and this is 1986!

"Most of the time, those patients aren't there voluntarily, but the point is, if that's where treatment is happening in that city, it shows how far we still have to go.

"The other people taking the tour that day were filled with amazement that ours was an open campus, that patients were free to come and go within the campus area.

"It isn't only out-of-towners who have odd ideas about alcoholics. The dietary staff asked if we were going to give the patients knives and forks, and as we were getting ready to open, we found ourselves fielding all kinds of questions from interested citizens. Was Eisenhower Medical Center going to have to increase the security on its campus? Was it safe to have so much glass in the buildings? They would say, 'Didn't you see *One Flew Over the Cuckoo's Nest?*' That was their image of alcoholics, that they were crazy and we were going to have to lock them up.

"When I was hired by Hazelden to run a hospital program, they brought me to Minnesota and had me enter as a patient for five weeks. They said, 'Even though you're not addicted, see how the steps of AA apply to your life.' And it was then I first started working the program for myself, accepting that I don't have control over how my life is going to go, and God does.

"It was a very good lesson. At the Betty Ford Center, we also put all our staff through treatment so they can get a feel for the patients' experience.

"By September 7, 1982, we had assembled a staff of twenty-four, and we proceeded to give them five weeks of intensive training. Hazelden sent a couple of people to help, and Betty came over the first day to meet everybody. She was wearing her hard hat because the buildings were still being finished. She shook every staff member's hand, and let them know how important they were in her eyes."

We were set to hold our Dedication ceremonies on October 3, and open our doors the following morning. A few days earlier, we scheduled what we referred to as a dry run, a phrase we thought was quite appropriate. A group of people from Eisenhower (nurses, nutritionists, bookkeepers), plus some of us alcoholics (volunteers from AA, and Leonard and I), came in for a test. We played the roles of patients, and the staff got to practice on us.

8

I have seen flowers come in stony places . . .

John Masefield

There were about twenty of us in the guinea-pig group for the dry run. We were asked to give our opinions of the food, the beds, the way the showers, as well as the therapy, worked. It was only for three days and two nights, but we all got an incredible boost out of the experience.

John Schwarzlose: "I had to decide who was going to room with Betty, and I picked a young therapist from Eisenhower Hospital. She was just kind of low-key. I didn't want someone who was going to sell her story to the *National Enquirer.* I also told the counselors, a couple of whom were quite intimidated by having Betty there, that they didn't have to get into deep therapy with her or Leonard."

Deep therapy or not—who had time for deep therapy?—Leonard and I were plenty busy. We were opening not only a new building but a new program, and everything had to be shaken down. Did the doors work? Were there bottlenecks at the food lines in the cafeteria? Were some of the instructional movies boring?

I was the Granny—there's a Granny for every residence hall

—and he or she is supposed to make sure everyone else does his or her job assignments. If you have a problem, you go to the Granny. If your bed isn't made correctly, the Granny is supposed to strip it. At least, they didn't make me clean the showers—at Long Beach, they made me clean the showers—but the idea of somebody who could never get anyplace on time being responsible for getting nineteen other people to places on time had its comic aspect.

We went through the whole drill, let the admissions people take our histories, signed a dozen different forms, checking for possible glitches in the routines. The counselors tested their lectures and tapes on the twenty of us, and we wrote out criticisms and turned them in. We didn't sign our names; we didn't dare.

One of the lectures I most admired was given by John Schwarzlose. It was on recovery. John said that, with a cold, you know you'll feel better in a few days, while with major surgery, you know it's going to take longer. But with a chronic disease—arthritis, diabetes, chemical dependency—there's no clear beginning, no clear end. You can't say, "On March 6, I got arthritis; on March 5, I didn't have it." It doesn't work that way.

He told us that alcoholics have to develop a continuing recovery plan, a blueprint for what's going to happen in our lives.

The world of treatment, as anyone who goes through it discovers, is unreal. You wish all that hugging and mutual support *did* go on in the real world, but it doesn't. Sitting around at night in your bathrobe with three other patients in bathrobes, all trading stories and life experiences, can be more important than group therapy, lectures, anything.

On the third day of our shakedown—we'd come in on a Tuesday and were going home on Thursday—we had a medallion ceremony. Ordinarily, at the Betty Ford Center, you get your medallion when you have completed your four or six weeks of treatment. Everyone in your hall comes, counselors and patients, and the bronze medallion—about the size of a half-dollar, with the serenity prayer on one side and the five-star emblem of General Eisenhower on the other—is passed from hand to hand.

Each person takes it and holds it, while saying something about the patient who is leaving.

We had guests come in for our medallion ceremony, people from Eisenhower, including President John Sinn, and his wife Joan. Some of our husbands and wives showed up too.

It was moving. A man—an administrator at Eisenhower who had been one of our pseudo patients—said, "I learned how to be myself here." And he thanked his counselor "for reminding me that in losing we win."

Not bad progress for three days' work.

Leonard's counselor said at first he'd thought Leonard was going to fly the coop. "I came to work at eight o'clock yesterday morning and here's this guy standing on the side of the road, and he had some long story about packing two pajama tops and no bottoms, or something, and his wife was bringing them. Whatever that was all about, you stayed with us, Len, and it's been good."

Leonard agreed. He said when the trustees had asked him and me to head up the task force to put this project together, we'd had three concerns: whether we could raise the money, how the physical plant we'd envisioned would work and whether we could get the right counselors and director, because without the right people, we wouldn't have anything.

"It looks to me," he said, "that we've got a terrific program. And what encourages me even more than my own thoughts is the fact that those non-alcoholics who were here for the past couple of days have been so impressed and thrilled and excited about what *they've* gone through."

At the end of the medallion ceremony, John Schwarzlose introduced "the head coach of our team, Joe Cruse," and as Joe walked up to the front of the room, one of the counselors yelled out, "Keep it short!" and Joe laughed along with everyone else and said, "After five weeks of training, they start getting sassy."

Joe said our counseling staff and support staff were like racehorses kicking at the gate, eager to break away, he spoke of patients having made reservations for next week, and then he talked directly to our guests. "You can see that in a very short

109

period of time, a real spiritual sharing can take place." He said lives were going to be "turned around in this place."

At the end of the program, we formed a circle, joined hands and said the Serenity Prayer. Contrary to what many people think, the Serenity Prayer did *not* originate with—or in—Alcoholics Anonymous. It's the work of the Protestant theologian Reinhold Niebuhr, an intellectual whose scholarly writings are not easily followed by the average reader. Yet this prayer is as clear and bracing as water from a mountain stream.

It reads:

> God grant me the Serenity
> to accept the things I
> cannot change;
>
> Courage to change the
> things I can; and
>
> Wisdom to know the
> difference.

Most support groups end each meeting with those words, but there are more. The prayer goes on:

> Living one day at a time;
> Enjoying one moment at a
> time; Accepting hardship
> as the pathway to peace;
>
> Taking, as He did, this
> sinful world as it is, not
> as I would have it;
>
> Trusting that He will make
> all things right if I
> surrender to His will;
>
> That I may be reasonably
> happy in this life, and
> supremely happy with Him
> forever in the next.
>   Amen.

110

And again, amen. To take the world as it is, one day at a time, is advice alcoholics need—it isn't bad advice for anybody—and I needed it more than most, as the medallion ceremony came to a close. It seemed to me there were still a million details that had to be taken care of before we could open this place.

It was the little things we might have forgotten that haunted me. We discovered the bathrooms were underequipped, and I went out to a shopping mall, Secret Service agents in tow, and ran around collecting soap dishes and toothbrush holders and glasses. There was no time to order them. It was like, we've got to get this thing done today, patients will soon be living in those rooms.

I had no anxiety about the big things. I knew we had great counselors; we'd interviewed extensively, and drawn them from all over the country—Minnesota, Louisiana, California—and we'd looked for the healthiest people we could find. Some were recovering alcoholics, some were not.

John Schwarzlose: "Alcoholism counseling is a big burnout field because people get so involved. I remember the first time one of my patients committed suicide. The guilt just over-whelmed me. It was in Peoria, a woman who was struggling in early recovery. She'd been sober seven or eight months, and she shot herself.

"You go through some terrible things. You think, if I had been a little more responsive, if I had done this or that. And then you're at the funeral, and nobody there knows you, the family doesn't know you. And you're crying, and everybody's wondering, who in the heck is this guy?"

It's the primary counselors who have the hardest job learning not to take their work home with them. They walk into a building every morning where they have seven to ten patients, each at a different place in his treatment, and what they must be able to say to those patients is: "I hear your pain, I understand your pain, but I can't take it over. It's yours. I want to help you feel it and then let go of it." Sometimes it's hard to make a new

111

counselor understand he can't save the world, he can only be a guide.

When I say we looked for people who were healthy, I don't mean people who didn't have problems, I mean people who were working on their problems, people who were growing emotionally. And we had got them. And now they were raring to go.

The night before the Dedication of the Betty Ford Center, Jerry and I went over there—it was already dark out—and walked through the three completed buildings: Firestone (administration), McCallum and West (residence halls). All the dignitaries who would be coming to the Dedication would also be offered a guided tour of the premises, and I wanted to make certain no doorknobs came off in their hands. My proud husband by my side, I wandered, switching lights on and off and straightening the pictures on the walls.

There was so much curiosity out there in the world about what we were doing, and I wanted it to be presented in the best possible way. It's funny to think of now, because the Center has changed so much since we first opened. As I've changed. As anything grows.

9

Do you know what it is as you pass
to be loved by strangers?

Walt Whitman

The day we opened, we admitted two patients, and three the day
after that. Within a week, McCallum Hall's twenty beds were
filled.

John Schwarzlose: "The way the Betty Ford Center took off
caught us all by surprise. We had high hopes, but we foresaw a
gradual growth, not a boom. And I watched Betty and wondered
how you stay humble when everybody's saying, 'Mrs. Ford, you
saved my life.' But she always saw that it was God working
through her. She said the way she had become First Lady had
been a stroke of fate, and this new chance to help other recovering alcoholics through her own recovery was also fate's interven-
ing.

"In the early days, she was a people pleaser. She couldn't tell
anybody no. Someone would call and say, 'Mrs. Ford, you may not
remember me, but I have this brother-in-law in New Orleans,
could you get him into treatment?' and she'd be on the phone to
me. 'We gotta get him in right now.' And I'd say, 'Betty, there's no
emergency in chemical dependency. If the guy needs medical

treatment, let's put him in an acute-care hospital, and as soon as we have a bed, we'll bring him here.'

"We don't push anybody aside in order to make room for apparent VIPs, or relatives of VIPs. Everybody goes on the same waiting list, and is notified when a bed comes free. We think Joe Schmoe who's out of work in San Diego is just as important as a friend of somebody on our board. Betty's expectation is that everyone gets VIP treatment at the Center.

"During the first year, we were feeling our way, trying to cope with so many things we hadn't expected. We'd thought we would fill up gradually, we'd thought most of our patients would be from southern California, we hadn't expected so much interest from men and women all across the U.S. and from many other countries.

"One day, Betty and I were touring the Center with some representatives from a large corporation, and one of them turned to her and said, 'This place is so beautiful, we're going to send our executives here.' And I was so proud of her. She looked at this man and said, 'Unless you'll send us your truck drivers, we don't want your executives.'"

Blame it on the Navy. I had taken my first, tentative steps toward getting well along with a crowd of sailors who didn't have trust funds. Pat Benedict, on whom I had leaned so much for strength and goodness of heart, spent her Thanksgivings in the barrio, feeding the homeless. And I was determined that our program not become a program for the rich and famous. It had to be for everybody, or it would not work.

Sometimes I thought it wasn't going to work anyway. We'd been going about six months when, at a meeting, the board asked John what kind of reports he was getting on how patients were doing. John said the reports were "fair," but there were a couple of local people who, after they got out, had used again very quickly. About local people, news travels fast. This disturbed me. I took every failure personally. I told the board I was worried. "It will hurt our reputation. It reflects on the Center, it reflects on me."

114

Leonard reached over and put his hand on my arm. "What if I worried," he said, "about every tire with my name on it that went bad?"

The group broke up laughing. But the Center's name has been burden, as well as honor. Because even if nobody else holds me responsible, I hold myself responsible.

A while ago, I went to a meeting of a support group, and a woman spoke up and said, "My husband and I are both alcoholics, and we went through Betty Ford." I cringed. At moments like that, I wonder why people can't say, "We went through treatment," but I'm fighting a losing battle. Even John refers to "Betty Ford." "Here at Betty Ford," he'll say to someone on the phone. And there's a group of alumni in New York who call the Center "Betty's place," as in "Have you got this month's newsletter from Betty's place?"

It's hard to make anyone understand what it's like to have your name on something, to be given credit for things you haven't done. I've been at meetings where someone turned and thanked me, and I hugged the person and said, "Don't thank me, thank yourself, you're the one who did it. With God's help."

From the beginning, we have wanted every patient at the Center to feel, "I'm important here, I have some dignity." The same with the counselors. We consider them as important as any doctors; they're the ones who are guiding our patients in treatment and recovery.

Alcoholic counseling isn't a very old field, and it hasn't been remunerative, either. We were determined to change that. Our counselors are well paid—not by the criteria of big business, but compared to the rest of the field—and we ask a great deal of them. Our standards are high. We won't interview a counselor unless he or she has had three full years' experience. We've been asked to franchise other centers, but that won't happen while I'm alive. It's enough to try to make this one the best it can be. When the Fisher building opens, that will give us eighty beds, twenty in each of four halls, and that's as many as we want.

Our staff cares. Along with the counselors, there are doctors, nurses, clergymen, psychologists, an exercise specialist, a nutritionist. Each patient has ten to fifteen people looking out for his needs.

But the patient still has to do the work. It's not easy for a sick person to understand. Everyone is used to going to a hospital and lying there while people do things to him. At the Center, we have to say over and over, "We're not going to do anything to you, not going to give you a shot, not going to give you a pill, not going to work any voodoo, you've got to do it. And if you listen, and watch, and let yourself feel, you'll find out how."

Some other places have more liberal guidelines—phones in the rooms, overnight passes, visitors seven days a week. We say, "Hey, you're not here to go on a pass." Our treatment is intensive. One magazine described us as a boot camp, which I don't think is fair. But we are serious about our program, it isn't a house party.

That's why the patient who wants to come here has to call our admissions office himself. We don't let your mother or your girlfriend or your husband put you in. You have to really want help. On the rare occasion when some chemically dependent person is coerced into treatment, it usually ends badly. I know of one young woman whose husband said he would leave her if she didn't sober up, so she came, filled with animosity, to us, and every night, when it was her turn to use the pay phone, she called her husband and complained. "They're a bunch of Moonies, they're brainwashing me, come and get me." That kind of thing is no good for the patient, and it's no good for the Center.

Patients have told me they have never felt so much concern and love as they get from the staff at BFC. Everyone who comes in has a complete physical examination given by Jim West, our medical director, or one of three other doctors. Within five days —once they've come to know the patient—the whole treatment team gets together to discuss the new arrival's individual problems. This group of therapists decides what to do, and how long it's going to take. Some people stay twenty-eight days, some stay six weeks. You have to be ambulatory, able to get around to classes, to meals, to lectures, before you can start treatment.

It isn't that we reject you if you're in withdrawal. Most patients are in some stage of withdrawal, but if the patient has a history of seizures or serious medical complications, he's put in an acute-care hospital. When the Betty Ford Center opened, we didn't take patients who had been using street drugs, though there were probably people who smoked marijuana. But the times change; many of our younger patients are now cross-addicted. In fact, cocaine is the second-leading drug of choice of our patients. You hear them at support group meetings saying, "I'm an addict-alcoholic."

In July 1983, the Betty Ford Center became a separate not-for-profit corporation. We had our own hospital license. We were still a subsidiary of the parent Eisenhower Medical Center, but now our board functioned independently, and we had our own budget. (Not-for-profit means if you collect more money than you spend, what's left over is put right back into the place.) All the donations sent to us—as distinguished from the fees charged by us—have gone for buildings and equipment, not for operating costs.

When we opened there was a tremendous amount of publicity attendant on our every move. Reporters swarmed to the campus, and it seemed as though we—Joe Cruse, John Schwarzlose, various counselors and I—were appearing on television shows, network and local, night and day. Finally, we called a halt. For one year, there was a moratorium on wisdom issuing forth from the Betty Ford Center. Partly because we didn't have the time to accommodate everyone who wanted to visit, partly because we needed to concentrate on the work we were doing and quit taking bows for how great we were. Especially since our greatness had yet to be proved.

I tried to stay on an even keel, and not be swept away by a vision of myself as "the lady with the lamp." I remember Leonard calling from New York one day to ask if I'd be willing to accept an award from the National Council on Alcoholism. He started telling me that my acceptance would be so helpful, such a benefit to mankind, stuff like that. "Ah, Leonard," I said, "you sound like all the rest of them. You know me too well to give me a lot of soft soap."

117

"Yeah, but it's true," he said. "If you show up, we will get a crowd."

"Okay," I said. "That's honest. But don't try and tell me how wonderful I am."

I couldn't afford to have Leonard—or Jerry or Meri Bell, any of the people closest to me—con me; there were enough strangers willing to lay on the flattery, and I'm as susceptible to sweet talk as the next one.

I had to keep remembering that while I was being written about and honored, there were volunteers over at the Center doing the dirty work. Nicky was one of them.

Nicky Firestone: "When Leonard went to treatment, it was a terrifically emotional experience. It just gave a different meaning to our lives. You look at something and think, my, that's interesting, why didn't I see it before?

"I was vitally interested in the development of the Betty Ford Center, but I didn't have any role in it. Then, after it opened, I signed up as a volunteer. That's the part I love more than anything. I just go over there and do what needs to be done.

"The patients and the counselors think I'm funny, they think I'm a nut. I hate messiness, so I pick up litter. They used to call me the Bag Lady because I'd go over with a big plastic bag and gather up whatever trash I could find. One day, I cleaned out the icebox, and that amused them very much.

"They tease me a lot, but the Center means so much to me, I just want it to be perfect. I feel very close to the counselors, I admire them tremendously, I admire their dedication. And I love to see the change in people who've gone through treatment. They come in, faces bloated, they're suffering the ravages of alcohol or drugs, and when you meet them again at an anniversary reunion, a year or two later, you don't recognize them. Even their facial expressions have changed.

"The uninitiated feel that alcoholism is a moral issue, a will-power issue. If you want to do something, by God, you can do it. I used to feel that way. But it has nothing to do with willpower.

118

When an alcoholic says to himself, 'I'm only going to have one drink tonight,' it doesn't work.

"Some people can't leave chocolate alone. If they have one piece, they have a box. But chocolate isn't going to kill you, or kill someone who gets in the way of your car.

"The thing that's hard to understand is that alcoholics don't want to do what they're doing. The periodic alcoholic is so contrite, so apologetic, he makes all kinds of promises, and means them from the bottom of his heart. And then it happens again. Until the drinker finally comes to the realization that he just can't touch alcohol.

"When somebody says to Leonard, 'Do you feel that you can never have another drink?' he says, 'I can have a drink anytime I want to, but I'm going to pay a price for it, and I don't know what the price will be, and it may even mean my life, so I'm not going to risk it.'

"He doesn't feel he's depriving himself, he feels he's saving himself. He doesn't drink, and he doesn't go out and take poison either.

"It was exciting to me when Leonard put up the money for Firestone Hall. I was happy he had the means to do it, and wanted to do it. I love to see money used in a good cause.

"And it is a good cause. I have been phoned by people at the Center and asked to come right over because someone thought I could help, and even though I was dressing for a dinner engagement, I've found myself saying, 'Why, certainly I'll be there.' I thought the heck with it, the dinner is not important. Life is tough. And people helping people is the only thing that I think is worth anything in this world today.

"It doesn't matter how tired you are, it doesn't matter what you're doing—you get mixed up in this racket and you're like a firehorse. You pull yourself together and run if you're needed. It is the most wonderful work."

Even when you believe with Nicky that the work is wonderful, you sometimes have to hang on with both hands. At the start, I would become anxious and resentful when I saw tabloids mock-

119

ing the idea of treatment. At least that's what it seemed to me they were doing. What else would you call a headline screaming out, "Big Star Goes to Betty's Booze Tank"? (That isn't exactly accurate, but it'll give you the idea.)

Eventually, I realized it didn't make any difference. Highly visible people in theater and television are role models, and if somebody comes to the Center because a well-known politician or movie star has said he or she got clean and sober there, then all the rest of it is unimportant. It doesn't matter by whose hand a life is saved. It's always the hand of God anyway.

Often, people are curious about how celebrities and the big rich mingle with the other patients. What if a big shot comes in and doesn't care to be part of the crowd? It's simple. If he doesn't settle in, he's asked to leave. Sometimes, somebody who thinks he is very important in business—or art—is unhappy when you tell him there will be no phone privileges for five days. He'll say, "Nobody is going to tell me that, I'm much too important not to have phone privileges for five days, the world can't go on without me." Then we say, "You'd better go back to the world and take care of it."

A woman is just as likely as a man to be guilty of false pride—think of my trying to former-First-Lady myself out of a four-bed room at Long Beach—and Leonard is fantastic at knowing how to cope with the wheeler-dealers. Because he was an industrialist, accustomed to power and money and a private plane, counselors at the Center send for him when they have a tough nut to crack, a newcomer who thinks he or she doesn't belong in a place with a bunch of commoners. I remember one lady who wanted Leonard to identify with her, and he did, but not in the way she expected. She was going on about how many racehorses she owned and how prominent she was, and Leonard shook his head. "Gee," he said, "I thought you were just another drunk like me."

Nicky, too, was unimpressed by the legends in their own minds. "I have a hard time with the high achievers," she said once. "I think it started when we were in the Embassy. I can't bear people who try to intimidate other people."

We've had patients who flunked treatment, so to speak, who

never earned their medallions, and sometimes it's nothing more than a snobbish attitude that gets in their way. One woman said her priest had urged her to go to Hazelden, but she'd said no way. "If I'm going anywhere, I'm going to Betty Ford, because she's like me." It was a kind of idea she had that I was a lady who drove around in a nice car. Poor silly woman. She could have got help anywhere. Or nowhere. Because help is help, and a drunk is a drunk. But unless she could break through her prejudice, she was not going to get well.

We've had celebrities who went through the Center and stayed clean and sober, we've had celebrities who left and drank and used again. Sometimes you get kind of snooty about your own recovery, and forget there are people who have to try more than once to find the sobriety that will give them long-term recovery. One top television executive who came to the Center went home and seemed to be doing well. Then he started using cocaine again. His station—in a major market—gave him leave, and I thought it was probably going to be a permanent leave. But I've since heard that he was going back to work, which gave me hope. He's a fine man, recovering from cocaine addiction.

We've had celebrities who were helpful to other patients, warm and loving and motherly, and celebrities who were a major pain. We've had celebrities who left the Center unchanged, and celebrities who experienced spiritual awakening.

One young woman, a very public figure who had been in treatment for a couple of weeks, became angry because her therapy group was beginning to focus on her, and she found that scary. She said, "I'm not putting up with this anymore," walked out of the group straight to the pay phone, and called the 800 toll-free number of one of the airlines.

"This is so-and-so," she said. "I want a flight to New York tonight." Now, an 800 toll-free number is probably handled out of a room with forty different operators, so the one you draw is left totally to chance. And this operator who picked up the phone said, "Oh, Miss so-and-so, I can't believe it's you. I'll get you the reservation in a second, but I need to tell you first that I've been in the AA program for almost eight weeks, really struggling, and when I found out you were in the Betty Ford Center, that gave me the reinforcement I needed to go on."

This patient of ours said, "Thank you, never mind the reservation," hung up the phone and walked back into group with tears streaming down her face. "I guess my Higher Power knows where I should be," she told the group. As John Schwarzlose says, "Anyone who can hear that and doesn't know God is in a place like this is missing the point."

Moving from the sacred to the profane, let me return briefly to the subject of money. The Center was built, the Center expanded. We want to be able to continually upgrade our program, by sending our counselors for advanced training, by improving our physical plant, and, in time, by providing a professional in-residence program. That takes money so I'm still putting the arm on anyone who will stand still long enough to listen to me. But it doesn't mean we gather up cash without looking at where it comes from.

John Schwarzlose: "Last year, a patient stuck a check for ten thousand dollars in my hand. It was made out to the Betty Ford Center, and this man said his company would double the donation. He was going to work it out with his accountant and his attorney. I returned the check. 'I appreciate this,' I said, 'but we can't take it until you are no longer a patient, and we figure that's a year after you leave here.'

"When I reported this exchange to our board, some of the members gulped, but everyone agreed that we could not afford to let a single thread of integrity be lost.

"A Medicare official came out to the Center and told Mrs. Ford and me that the government would only pay for sixteen to twenty-one days of treatment, and he asked how we would handle that. Betty said, 'We'll swallow the rest of it.' 'What?' the guy said. 'If a person needs twenty-eight days, that's how long he'll stay,' Betty said. 'We'll find a way to cover it.'

"For me, it's worthwhile to work here, knowing Betty and the other people on the board stand up for what they believe.

"During that first year she was still somewhat of a people

pleaser, grateful that the BFC had been built, busy thanking everyone. But early on, she really began to emerge as president. She became a part of the regular in-patient and out-patient lecture series, and began to spend time with patients. She wanted to know everything they went through in a day, what they thought needed to be changed.

"She never interferes with treatment, but she will spend hours in the coffee lounge kibitizing with patients.

"We have a meeting on the first Monday of every month, a meeting with all the clinical counselors. Betty often comes to that. In the beginning, she took home organizational charts and worked on them. I'd get a call at ten o'clock at night, and it would be Betty asking questions."

There were high points in those early days. When we discovered we needed an additional building which could also serve as a family treatment center, John, Leonard and I flew down to San Diego to talk to Joan Kroc about it. Joan, the widow of Ray Kroc, the founder of McDonald's and owner of the San Diego Padres, is a philanthropist who's given away millions. She is not only generous; she is highly respected among those working in the field of alcohol and drugs.

In 1976, she established Operation Cork (Cork is Kroc spelled backwards), a program to educate the public about chemical dependency and its impact on the family. Joan gave us a huge check and we used it to help build our Cork Family Pavilion.

Large contributions and small, we have welcomed every one. We offer twelve scholarships a year, and we take twelve charity cases a year. We help families who can barely afford to put a patient through treatment, let alone come to the family program themselves. We get funds from foundations, from alumni, from individuals who have lost family members to alcoholism, from individuals who have *almost* lost family members to alcoholism.

Two years into my sobriety, my husband gave me a pink-and-white piggy bank for Mother's Day. A note stuck out of the slot. It said, "This is my Mother's Day recognition for my First

123

Lady." And inside the note, there was a check to the Center. The pig and the note are still on my desk. They show the kind of support I've had.

About a year after I quit drinking, Jerry stopped too. He came home from a plane trip one night, and I said, "A nightcap will relax you. Let me make you one." And he said, "No, thanks." "Come on," I said. "It will make you feel so much better, and I really don't mind." He said no. "I don't want one."

I was puzzled. "We always used to have a nightcap before we went to bed."

"Yeah," he said. "And I never really enjoyed it."

I was even more puzzled. "Then, why did you do it?"

"Because," he said, "I didn't want you to drink alone."

Right or wrong, mistaken or not, it shows the kind of support I've had.

The dedication of the Betty Ford Center, October 3, 1982. The dais guests included: (from left) Joan Sinn, John Sinn, Bob Hope, Barbara Bush, Vice President George Bush, Dolores Hope, Nicky Firestone, Leonard Firestone. [Photo courtesy of the Eisenhower Medical Center.]

Above left, Jerry and I reviewing the plans for a new inpatient building at the Betty Ford Center. [Photo by Harry Benson.] Above right, some of my friends who have been most important to me in my recovery: Leonard Firestone, John Schwarzlose, Ann Cullen and, sitting, Meri Bell Sharbutt, April 1986. [Photo by Alice Springs.]

Jerry and I are very fortunate to have four children who became such fine adults. (Mike, top, Jack, left, Steve, right, and Susan Ford Vance.) [Photo by Russ Ohlson.]

Our precious granddaughters: Heather, Tyne, Hannah, Sarah and Bekah—all innocence at Christmas. The rest of the year, watch out! [Photo by Russ Ohlson.]

One of the happiest days of my life. I'm smiling because Jerry is about to announce that he won't be seeking the GOP nomination, March 1980. [Photo by Chuck Scardino. Courtesy of Desert Sun Newspapers.]

Roslyn Carter, Diane Sawyer and I prepare for an interview in the reproduced Oval Office at the Gerald R. Ford Museum in Grand Rapids, Michigan, April 1984. [Photo courtesy of the Gerald R. Ford Museum.]

I was induced to join Bob Hope in a soft-shoe routine for the dedication of the Gerald R. Ford Museum. In this rehearsal it was no-shoe. [Photo by Anna Moore Butzner. Courtesy of the Grand Rapids Press.]

My dedication to the cause of women's rights was probably sparked by the independent, caring women who have filled my life. Above, left, Hortense Neahr Bloomer Godwin. Above right, Dolores Hope. [Photo by David Hume Kennerly]. Below, Martha Graham. [Photo by David Gould].

10

I was, being human, born alone;
I am, being woman, hard beset;
I live by squeezing from a stone
The little nourishment I get.

Elinor Wylie

The emotional support I've been talking about is not there for all women.

These are the statistics I have heard. Nine out of ten women stay with their alcoholic husbands. Nine out of ten men abandon their alcoholic wives.

Not only did Jerry not abandon me but I have also been the recipient of a great deal of goodwill from strangers. Many have a feeling of understanding based on shared tribulation.

Somebody once said to me, "These days, you seem to be even more popular than your husband," and I said, "Well, my husband didn't have all the trials that I had." When I go through crowds, I have to be careful, because a woman will come up and give me a hug or grab my arm and say, "You know, we're recovering from the same disease," and frankly, I don't know which disease she's talking about, cancer or alcoholism or arthritis.

Whichever one it happens to be, I always hope she isn't trying to squeeze nourishment from a stone, but has a husband like mine. For a while after my mastectomy and the subsequent chemotherapy, I grappled with low self-esteem. I've never been very secure anyway—if I walked into a room, I was always sure that half the people there didn't like me. And losing a breast makes you feel disfigured psychologically as well as physically, less adequate as a marriage partner. You've failed to live up to the physical perfection you've wanted, not just for yourself (you can live without it) but for your husband.

My operation came at a time when some women were going without underclothes and wearing sheer blouses. Everywhere I traveled, I was aware of beautifully built females, and I suffered over having let my husband down.

To Jerry, this was nonsense. He was always reinforcing me—"Oh, you're much more beautiful than she is." In more than thirty years, he has never belittled me or made me feel I was inadequate—even when I was taking pills and drinking—and that's unusual. At support group meetings, or over at the Center, I hear women say, "I have lost my family. My husband couldn't stand to be around me. My children would not come home."

So many women had individual problems that the Center was not very old before we made some changes. It was Dan Anderson, the president of Hazelden, who steered us in a new direction. We had opened West Hall a month after McCallum, and North Hall after that. All the buildings were coed, until Dan came out and looked us over. His review was mixed.

In a conversation with John Schwarzlose and me, he said, "You're doing a great job, but do you want to be just another sixty-bed treatment center? You have an opportunity to do something special here. There are clinical differences between alcoholic men and women that need to be addressed in treatment, and because of Betty's reputation, half your patients are women. Why not separate them from the men?" (Hazelden was then the only treatment place we knew of that practiced this separation.)

Dan said he could foresee the day "when the Betty Ford Center could become a standard-bearer, known for providing good chemical-dependency services to women. Services they haven't had in the past."

In that meeting, it was clear to us that he was making sense, so we talked to our board of directors and our professional staff to find out how they felt about the idea. The staff split nineteen to nineteen, and I broke the tie. It was decided West Hall would be an all-women's building, and we've never backed off from that decision.

Yes, we got some arguments. All of the staff, as you can tell by the split vote, was not entirely open to the idea. They questioned why women needed anything different from the regulation treatment that men were getting. Even trained counselors did not always comprehend the greater anger, the more intense feeling of resentment women have about being alcoholic.

Alcoholism had always been a macho disease. "It's a good man's failing," the Irish used to say. When he comes of age, a man is supposed to learn to drink, and he can drink a lot—go to lunch, have a couple of martinis, drink after work—and still get his job done. A woman can't have a small child and be drinking. Not if she wants society to accept her as a good mother.

Most of the treatment centers across the country had been geared to men. Men were the ones who came forth, admitted they were alcoholics. They went into treatment—their bosses sent them, or they sent themselves—because they found their ability to make a living threatened, whereas women drank at home, hidden and protected by their families. They didn't find their way to treatment. And the few who did often resented—as I had done to some extent at Long Beach—the fact that it was a man's treatment.

Fortunately for me, the group of women from Laguna—Muriel Zink, Pam Wilder, several more—came in from the outside and shared. They made the early steps of my recovery less shaky and less threatening. It was comforting just to be with other recovering women.

I know my friends and I were not engaging in something unheard of before the mid-1970s. I know a lot of women who have been recovering for twenty, thirty years. But twenty years ago, a woman who went to treatment received treatment that focused on men. Even the big book of Alcoholics Anonymous was slanted toward men.

Twenty years ago, most women just toughed it out, tried to straighten up on their own, for fear of shaming their children or endangering their husbands' jobs. The same way many women have to work twice as hard as men to prove themselves in the business world, so I think these women had to work twice as hard to gain their sobriety.

Women aren't weak. Bearing children, rearing them, running a household can't be done by weaklings. Neither can recovering from alcoholism. But over the centuries, a stereotype developed of what a woman was supposed to be, a creature on a pedestal whose man would carry all of life's burdens on his broad shoulders. One who didn't need to think; her thinking would be done for her. With no cares, how could such a creature be depressed, or uncertain about who she was?

This is who she was. Somebody's daughter, somebody's mother, somebody's wife. Her identity as an individual was almost nonexistent.

Stephanie Covington, a specialist in female alcoholism and sexuality, developed a workshop project that is very interesting. She asks a group to imagine that, as they are growing up, most of the voices they hear on radio and television are the voices of women, that the bases of power and economic strength rest in the hands of women, that the government is administered by a wise, all-knowing woman.

After establishing these ground rules, Stephanie asks her students for their reactions. Generally, the women express feelings of strength and power and pride, the men express feelings of fear and confusion and helplessness.

And one hopes, at the end, a little enlightenment.

Women have been receiving negative messages all their lives, and they bring negative attitudes with them when they come to treatment. They have lived in the stereotype of what they should be as women. And when they cannot achieve everything that the role demands, they are quick to believe there is something wrong with them. Only now are we beginning to see that perhaps the error was not in them, but in the stereotype. The distorted vision is changing, but it may take a long long time.

The female alcoholic has more emotional problems, more health problems, more parenting problems, makes more suicide attempts, than the alcoholic man. The female alcoholic can endanger her unborn baby because of alcohol and drugs passed through the umbilical cord. Prenatal exposure to high levels of chemicals can cause death through spontaneous abortion or stillbirth, as well as malformation, growth deficiency, retardation. This fetal alcohol syndrome is the third leading cause of birth defects.

Women alcoholics have to deal with other physical problems too. Our bodies have more fat tissues than men's. This means we absorb drugs and alcohol more rapidly, and have more toxic reaction to a given amount of alcohol. Our internal organs are more susceptible to the damage that can be done by chemicals we use. The changes in a woman's estrogen level can heighten and prolong the effect of alcohol. The mood swings that may accompany hormonal changes can be intensified by using chemicals. More women than men experience sexual dysfunction. Many use alcohol to overcome this, to relax, loosen up. Unfortunately, alcohol is a depressant and an excessive amount of it will only heighten any already existing dysfunction.

There is an adage in recovery that says, "If you don't want to slip, stay away from slippery places." That's easier for men than for women. Men don't *have* to go back to the bars where they got in trouble, they don't *have* to phone the cocaine dealer. But in a large percentage of cases, a woman's slippery place was her own kitchen, her bedroom, her bathroom. And the people around her when she was drinking or using weren't pushers, they were the members of her family. After she leaves treatment, she is returning to her slippery places and the very same conditions under which she came to grief. She has to learn to be wary, if she's going to be able to continue with her recovery.

There are still women out there who are afraid to ask for help, but fewer than there used to be, in this age of assertiveness training, and female doctors and lawyers and bank presidents and airline pilots and members of the plumbers' union.

There have, of course, always been women who went into

the marketplace, some from necessity, some from ambition. But in the past, it was no easier for the alcoholic working woman to get help than it was for her housebound sister.

Because in the boss-employee situation you found old boys talking man to man. "Bud, I'm worried about you, you're getting behind in your work, and a lot of days you don't come back after lunch," etc. With a woman, it was more embarrassing. Rather than confront her, they'd fire her.

The average woman who comes to the Betty Ford Center is forty-four years old, married, has children and a job. (We've had them from eighteen to eighty-four.) And she does better in therapy when her group is all-female. In a group that is coed, we have found, she tends to remain in the nurturing role of mother or wife, she hangs back, urging the men to do all the talking.

In an all-women's group, she's not allowed to sit back. Another woman will say to her, "What about *you?* How is this affecting *you?* How do *you* feel?"

There are also intimidating subjects, personal subjects—sexual abuse, incest—that women are more comfortable talking about with other women. They're fearful of expressing their anger about these things in front of men. Besides, they're still trying to please men. So, although there are exceptions to every rule, women don't get well as fast in mixed groups.

The woman alcoholic is less apt than a man to be caught driving while drunk, she is less apt to be arrested on the street, less apt to end up in jail, and she has a much better chance than a man of dying without ever having her disease diagnosed.

At least a third—and maybe half—of the alcoholics alive today are women.

One of the reasons I started openly discussing my own recovery was that I was so flabbergasted by what I had learned about the extent of women's dual dependencies on alcohol and prescription drugs. Eighty percent of American women who are alcoholic—more likely the ones over forty—are also dependent on one or more prescription drugs. And that chemical combination is explosive.

Another reason I started talking (when many felt I should

keep quiet) was my mother. I've said that my mother was strong and kind, but she was also free, a liberated woman, as was her mother before her, so it was inevitable that I would grow up to be vocal about women's issues. My mother cared for three children practically by herself. When she went to work selling real estate during the depression, it was a perfectly ladylike thing to do, but nobody in her set had ever done anything like it.

Eleanor Roosevelt was another important role model for me. I admired her ability to speak out in support of her beliefs, although I didn't always agree with the causes she championed. I wouldn't be surprised if Mrs. Roosevelt had also fueled my mother's independent and self-confident way of thinking.

While I was still at Long Beach, I got a letter from an elderly cousin who said he knew I was going to make it because my forebears had the right stuff. He said he had always thought of my mother "not only as one of the nicest persons I ever knew, but also as a person who overcame the rough times."

That stayed in my mind when I started trying to do something about female alcoholics. I didn't need a cause. I was already involved in raising money for the American Cancer Society, and the Arthritis Foundation, and mental health and underprivileged children. But the plight of alcoholic women pulled at me.

Sometimes, as I've mentioned before, I'm called over to the Center and asked to talk with a woman who thinks she's too well-bred to be an alcoholic and doesn't realize she has just come from different circumstances, that she is just another child of God, that her problem is not so different from the problem of the young girl who's been prostituting herself on the street to get drugs. The girl on the street simply hasn't had the advantage of being able to get her stuff legally, from doctors.

Still, I don't push myself on people. When I do one-on-one counseling, it's because a patient has asked for me. I am not qualified to be a professional counselor—what I don't know about medical matters is a large amount—but I can answer a cry for help.

If a woman has had a mastectomy, and she's having a hard time because she's never come to terms with it, I can share with her my own knowledge of that experience. Her mastectomy is an issue that's separate from her drinking, but in recovery from either, sexual anxieties abound.

The mastectomy may have made the woman feel physically undesirable, and the drinking may have made it possible for her to accept herself as a sexual being. Some women have never gone to bed with their husbands without having taken a few drinks or pills, so they are terrified of what the adjustment will be when they go home from treatment. They are afraid they will fail at sex.

You counsel them not to expect it to be easy, to take the time to get comfortable, because everything's different in abstinence. You assure them that this burden of guilt they are carrying around because they've caused so much trouble will eventually go away.

And you hope that it means something to them, because you believe they can make it.

A woman alcoholic who gulps her sherry out of the kitchen cupboard is, medically speaking, as much at risk as the woman alcoholic who does her tippling at a singles bar. Though, philosophically speaking, the woman in the singles bar is more apt to lose her reputation along with her liver. Because the double standard still exists. If a man goes into a bar, has a drink, watches a football game, tells some lies to some other men, nobody thinks anything of it. If a woman goes into a bar, she's looking for trouble.

The French writer Simone de Beauvoir declared in her book *The Second Sex* that feminine characteristics were socially acquired. "One is not born, but rather becomes a woman," she said. "It is civilization as a whole that produces this creature, intermediate between male and eunuch, that is described as feminine."

Whether or not you want to sign off on that, it is nonetheless true that we have a civilization that doesn't like to admit nice women drink, a civilization in which the idea of an alcoholic woman's needing special attention is still fairly new.

Not only employers and uneasy husbands have turned their backs on the fact of women alcoholics, so have doctors.

Muriel Zink: "I went to my own physician and said, 'I believe I'm an alcoholic,' and he said, 'Muriel, what's it going to be next, Zen Buddhism?' A lot of professional people attached so much stigma to the idea of alcoholism that, in their minds, a woman who drank too much was disgracing motherhood, apple pie, and America.

"My husband was the same way. If I got tight, he would be right there with the excuses. 'Louis really loaded your drink,' or 'You were very tired,' or 'It wasn't good liquor,' or 'You haven't been eating right.'

"A friend from New York who had quit drinking came to a party beside our pool, and I made her iced tea. Because I was going to protect her from temptation. Another guest, the wife of a movie director, said, 'You must try the daiquiris, they're absolutely marvelous.' And my friend said, 'No, thank you, the iced tea will be just fine.' And the director's wife kept raving about the daiquiris—'They put something in them that makes them taste like almonds—' and finally my friend said, 'No, thank you, I don't drink, I'm an alcoholic.'

"I was horrified. I took my friend aside and apologized for the director's wife, and my friend said, 'Honey, it's all right, I have a hard time not letting everybody know I'm an alcoholic,' and I thought, oh, my God, she's had brain damage.

"But she was the friend I called when I finally admitted I had a problem. 'I think I'm an alcoholic,' I said. She didn't say, 'It took you a long time to see it.' She said, 'Well, honey, try it on for size. Wear it like a loose garment. You know, we get what we need when we need it.' "

Sometimes, what women need is the help of other women. A patient at the Center remembers, "I walked in frightened, and I discovered a lot of women as frightened as I was. That made it easier. It was a case of 'Coward, take my coward's hand.' "

One well-known entertainer has described recovery as "belonging to this big huge club. Recovery is a unique process and people who are successful in recovery have a camaraderie, we

133

have a little edge on 'normal' people. You can't survive out here without that connection."

The fellowship of recovering women cuts through all kinds of barriers. I read in a book called *A Woman Like You* testimony from a woman who identified herself as Lulu F.

"Even when I go to meetings now," she said, "there often aren't black people unless I bring them with me. But it just doesn't bother me. I talk and share just the same because AA works no matter what the color of your skin. I was never taught to be prejudiced. But when you're looking for an excuse not to change, the first excuse the black person has is 'I can't identify with or relate to those white people.' I heard Betty Ford talk one time, and we felt exactly the same way; she just had more money to spend than I did. Thank God I didn't have it, or I would have been dead."

Most of us female alcoholics do feel "exactly the same way." To sum up, we feel guilty because we haven't been able to fulfill the role society has established for us, we feel depressed by our failures and our inability to cope without chemicals, we feel angry because we lost control of our lives. The disease impacts on women faster and more intensely, so when we finally seek help—and we hide in our denial longer than men do—we're sicker, physically and emotionally. Once we leave treatment, we may need intensive aftercare. But what we will have learned is that, wherever we go, there will be other women who will understand.

For a long time, despite my previously stated interest in women's issues, the women in my life always played secondary roles. I had girlfriends in school and while I was working, but like most young women, I preferred to be with men. Later, the women I knew were more or less appendages of men who were friends of my husband. We came along with the men, we shared a very little of our lives with each other.

Since my treatment—and within my recovery—I have learned how wonderful and special women are. We're a unique and sometimes mystifying breed, and I am reminded of this every time I go to the Center and talk with the women patients.

One of those patients, a friend who went through treatment last year, gave me her diary and said I could use it any way I liked. She and I both thought a few pages might give the reader an idea —if only a sketchy one—of what a patient's first days are like. She lived in West Hall.

11

Nine P.M. Bed. A book, V. Woolf's letters. Lights out, sleep not quite right
away. No Valium. The night passes in
black chiffon.

James Schuyler

Monday: Camp Betty. That's what they call it.

I read in *Parade* magazine how this rehab consisted of patient units that rival "luxurious condominium accommodations."
Right. But in luxurious condominium accommodations, you don't
generally have some guy come and take away your hair dryer to
see if you're hiding stuff in it. They also take away your vitamin
pills and aspirin and certainly anything stronger than aspirin that
you have been foolish enough to bring.

Got in late, almost 4 P.M., and met my roommate. Fresh-
faced kid, but she has been doing drugs since she was twelve.
Lots of acid. She is the Granny for our hall, and right now she is
outside bellowing, "Circle!" I wander out to see what this means.
What it means is that before supper—or any other activity—we,
all twenty of us on the hall, go out the front door and form a big
circle, arms around each other's shoulders, and recite the Serenity Prayer.

Supper is at 5:10 P.M., so early I wonder when these people
have lunch. The cafeteria is big and bright and two women invite

137

me to sit with them. I notice the men from North Hall seated together. It is explained to me that the women's hall and the men's hall do not mingle. You not only don't eat with the men, you aren't supposed to sit with them at lectures, or hang out with them at night. No fraternization allowed.

There's another new girl today. She is not nervous like me, or maybe she is nervous, but she could be a stand-up comic. She says she was shocked when the authorities took away her mouthwash and her perfume. After that, a counselor said, "Come on, Eve, I'll take you to your room, you're in the Swamp." (The Swamp is what they call the four-bed room.)

"They think I'm going to drink my perfume," she says. "And they sleep in a swamp. These people are crazier than I am."

After supper, there's a lecture by John Schwarzlose, who runs this place. He tells us 85 to 90 percent of the people in the United States who need treatment will never get it.

Won't their families help? No, the family's denial is as strong as the patient's.

Won't the doctor help? No, he's not trained in chemical dependency. He couldn't fix your car either.

What about your clergyman? No, he's more apt to lay a sin trip on you, tell you if you'd been going to church, you wouldn't have ended up in here.

When I get back to my room, I am supposed to write down my daily feelings in a notebook to be turned in to my counselor the next morning. We have been given so many books to read, questionnaires to fill out, things to think about, I don't know how I am going to be able to do a written assignment too. And I want to keep this diary, just so I'll remember what I saw and heard and felt when I was here.

"Feelings" is a big thing in this place. There must be people who can't express any feelings whatever, because the kit of materials we are issued includes a whole list of "feeling" words to draw from. Like for anger, we're given "contemptuous," "resentful," "irritated," "grumpy" and, I swear, twenty-four more!

Well, I'm feeling grumpy. But I think it is only that I am very tired from the long day, and overwhelmed by the amount of

138

reading I am expected to finish, and tomorrow I hope to be more cheerful. The women on this hall are very sweet with each other, and there is a good feeling of comradeship and a lot of gallows humor.

I am worried that I have to go through a physical, which I always find embarrassing, tomorrow.

Tuesday: They get you up at the crack of dawn. Breakfast is at 7:20, and then you have to walk for almost an hour, and then there's a lecture. Three lectures a day, morning, afternoon and evening.

I have a blinding headache and go to the nurse to ask for a pill—any pill. I am turned down.

Anyway, I'm in the right place for my physical examination (it's very thorough, thorough enough so I miss the 9 A.M. lecture), and at ten there's group therapy.

The members of my group include a fashion plate, an anorexic redhead and a middle-aged lady with a broken arm who says she is not an alcoholic. There is also an intellectual whose vocabulary is awesome, and a woman who seems so regal I can't imagine her tipsy, no matter how I try.

We discuss our chemical dependencies. Intellectual says she always kept a flask in her office, Regal says she always had brandy in her car, Anorexic says she was always out looking for fixes. Broken Arm remains serene. "This doesn't refer to me, I didn't drink at all during the day."

Our counselor, a soft-voiced, gentle woman, asks Broken Arm why she persists in her denial. "Your family brought you here because they love you, and they say you drink a fifth a day, and take sleeping pills."

Broken Arm is not impressed. "Everything they said is not necessarily true. I *did* take sleeping pills, and I *did* drink two shots of whiskey every night. But I did *not* wet the bed, and I did *not* have to be picked up off the floor."

"You're fighting something," the counselor says. "Quit fighting. Surrender."

This counselor is fantastic. Very pale-skinned, wears frilly blouse, but nothing frilly about the way she hooks right into every patient, kind, but direct, her eye is like a laser. She says the first year she counseled, "it was sink or swim. I got so involved with my patients, I was available to them twenty-four hours a day. Now I have a kind of shield around myself."

She says we all "use" for a quick fix, to be able to walk through the pain, walk through the fear.

This is an exciting day. I can't believe how fast you start to care about twenty strangers. You form a bond that's almost mystical, and it happens in a matter of hours.

Several times a week, the Center brings in AA meetings. At the beginning of a meeting, they go around the lecture hall and everyone gives his or her name. "I'm so-and-so, I'm an alcoholic." "I'm so-and-so, I'm an addict-alcoholic." Whatever. When they get to Broken Arm, she looks up brightly. "I'm so-and-so," she says, "and I'm not an alcoholic. Yet."

One guy gets up and says, "Cocaine loves me."

Another patient gets up and says he's afraid when he goes back to work—he works in a hospital—"they won't trust me with the keys to the narcotics cupboard." I'm sitting there thinking, well, I should hope not.

There's a man who's been drinking forty years, and says he didn't want to come into treatment until he'd emptied his liquor cabinet. He says, "Nobody else is going to drink my brandy."

After the meeting is over, a woman from our hall announces, "I've had such a good time, I can't remember when I've had such a good time," as though she's been to the movies, and the man who is leading the meeting says fine. "When you go home, call AA."

My head still hurts, but I am happy. I like the safety and the structure, of which there hasn't been much in my life, and the process. I really have begun to love these people. I have worked hard for a long time at the cost of having no personal relationships. Or maybe because I wanted to avoid personal relationships. Except with scotch, or Demerol. I feel myself becoming humanized.

140

Wednesday: These days are almost too packed. If you can grab five minutes to go outside your room and sit on your terrace or patio or whatever they call it and look up at the mountains, and smell the trees, it stretches your soul, but those breaks don't come often. Every afternoon, in addition to lecture and exercise —sometimes aerobics, sometimes pool—and book study, there is also a medallion ceremony for "graduating" patients.

Today, little B. got her medallion. She is on my hall, but not in my group, and I like her a lot. She is as crazy as I am. Goes into the pool in tights, so nobody can see her fat thighs. She is leaving tomorrow, and everyone here thinks she is going to be fine, but she is going back to a domineering husband, and I worry about her. I also worry about whether my roommate has the will to stay off drugs. Does this mean there is still hope for me as a connected-to-others human being?

Little B. says at medallion ceremony that she had thought for a long time her counselor didn't like her, because he always seemed to disappear when she had a problem. "I didn't want you to lean too hard," her counselor tells her now. "I didn't want you to ascribe any magic to me, because I'm only an alcoholic, just like you."

Today, for the first time since Broken Arm has been here, she wasn't totally negative in group. The counselor said, "What do you think of the treatment here?" and she said, "Some of it is nice."

Thursday: The cocaine addicts get to use the pool at night. They're hyperactive, and it's supposed to calm them down. There's a certain amount of fussing from people who would *like* to use the pool at night but are just plain old alcoholics, so find it off limits.

Following are a few interesting things I've heard in lectures these past four days:

Shame and guilt are different. Shame is "I am bad." Guilt is "I have done something bad." (I'm still working on that.)

Depression is anger turned inwards, and can result in arthritis, colds, flu, cancer, heart attack.

141

Dr. West, who's the medical director here, lectured on the personality of the alcoholic. He said alcoholics have low tolerance for frustration, they are woundably sensitive, and they are isolated. "You have to break out, take the risk," he said. He also said there was no such thing as returning to limited use of alcohol or drugs. "If one day, fifteen years from now, you see a drunk and say, 'Oh, how awful. *I'm* not like that anymore,' it won't be true. You're just not *doing* it anymore."

And he told us there are two things necessary for mental health. (1) You must have a sense of your own worth. (2) You've got to relate to at least one other human being openly, unconditionally and unguardedly. If you lack either of these, you're mentally ill.

At the end of his talk, Dr. West promised something beautiful. "In recovery," he said, "we're given floods of grace."

We are kept very busy here. We are given no time to look at a newspaper, watch TV (except on weekends, they tell me), listen to music. We are supposed to spend every moment possible "interacting," because addicted people are egocentric babies, and we have to be forced to focus on other people.

Before you leave treatment, you're supposed to write your autobiography, and then gather your therapy group together in the lounge and make them listen to it.

The lounge is nice, there are easy chairs and plants and a big fireplace, and up two steps, there's a coffee machine, and cold drinks and fruit, but for three nights now, I've seen Intellectual trying to drum up an audience. You think you're afraid to share your guilty secrets with others, because they'll listen with sick fascination and then spread the news all over town. Then you find out that you can't *force* others to come listen to them. That really struck me funny.

Everybody is so exhausted by evening, and they have their own journals to write. If you can stay awake past nine o'clock, you find yourself sitting up pretty much alone. Even people who are used to sleeping pills are falling asleep without them.

142

Friday: A counselor on the evening staff has given me an assignment. I am to share my chemical-use history with six peers and ask them for feedback. I am supposed to record the chemicals I have used in my life, the amounts I used, the frequency with which I used, run this past my peers and record the insights I gain from the exercise. I can only buttonhole four peers. (What? Only four people want to hear about the night I had my stomach pumped?) But I lay out my whole sorry saga, and one at a time they point out that I'm not a damn bit different from anyone else. I have fears, low self-esteem, I want to be admired, drugs and liquor make me feel less scared and more likable.

When I get back to our room, my compassionate roommate has brought me a chocolate bar. It tastes fantastic. I feel accepted.

Today in group, it was Intellectual's turn in the "hot seat." She is told by the rest of the group that she's melodramatic, judgmental, manipulative, a self-justifier, willful, sorry for herself, angry, aggressive and threatening, as well as smart and talented and likable. She agrees with most of this, and says she took drugs to "quiet down the frenzy."

She is told she mustn't talk for twenty-four hours. Not to anybody. Not a word. A plaque is hung around her neck to advise passersby not to engage her in conversation.

"In recovery," the counselor says, "we have to keep things simple. They tell you when you go home, if you do the first step of AA perfectly, you will not use or drink again."

Well, it's easy to admit you're powerless over alcohol and drugs and your life has become unmanageable when you're safe in here, because you get a lot of reinforcement; outside, it won't be so simple.

During this week, I have had meetings with a psychologist and a clergyman. The clergyman says he's not here to push religion down people's throats, but to help people to the spirituality of the program, and to seek a power outside themselves. He is a recovering alcoholic, and it took him a long while to get the message because he didn't identify with other alcoholics. "*I* didn't have a divorce, *I* didn't abandon my children, *I* wasn't a skid row bum."

143

Identifying is the crux. In one meeting, a woman says, "This sounds snobbish, but I don't relate to a bunch of farm women bawling because a cow kicked over the pail," and the counselor says, "Try to relate to the *feelings* of those women, not to the women. Don't you relate to disappointment? Dashed expectations?"

Tonight, they brought in some alumni of the Betty Ford Center for a panel discussion in the lecture hall. The first man said he came to treatment to save his marriage. "But it wasn't like the TV ad. 'John, I think you've been drinking too much.' 'Yes, but it's all right, dear, I've signed up to go to Betty Ford.'"

An alumnus who's skin and bones—he was twenty pounds thinner when he was on drugs—says nobody who's recovering should plunge into an emotional relationship for at least a year, because you're just not strong enough. Lots to think about. Almost too much to think about.

What a week. Games, exercises, lessons, lessons, lessons. Sermons in stones. Next week, I'm planning to be stronger, smarter, and maybe I'll even understand more of the things I'm being told. I asked one middle-aged lady why she had chosen to come here, rather than going someplace else, and she said it was because of Mrs. Ford. "I once heard Betty Ford speak," she said. "And there was such a look of serenity and peace on her face. And I thought, if I could get that look, I would be happy."

I saw Mrs. Ford briefly today—she came and talked to the patients—and I told her what the lady had said because I thought it would please her. "She doesn't know how long it took me to get that look," she said.

12

Independence? That's middle-class
blasphemy. We are all dependent on
one another, every soul of us on earth.

George Bernard Shaw

I was not struck with "a look of serenity and peace" on my way
home from treatment. I had to struggle, one day at a time, to
maintain my balance. We all have to. But it can be done.

It's hard for the chemically dependent person to believe
there is life without substance abuse. Any addict who's tried to
stop drinking or using for a day, or even a few hours, and who, as
a result, gets the shakes or the screaming meemies or simply
suffers from a sense of impending doom, thinks, there's no way I
can make it.

You can make it. But it's easier if you don't have to do it
alone.

In an essay she wrote back in 1951, Katherine Anne Porter
talked about the richness of the relationship "between a man and
a woman who are good lovers, good friends and good parents;
who belong to each other, and to their children, and whose children belong to them: that is the meaning of the blood tie that
binds them, and may bind them sometimes to the bone."

Gorgeous writing, but a simple thought. Belonging is necessary to most of us ordinary human beings. And in recovery, you

begin to belong again, you come out of the isolation where you lived with—and for—your particular drug, and rejoin the world.

But you have to learn belonging means being part of, not owning or being owned. I see it with my children. I've let go. Today, I don't try to control my children. They have their lives, and what they choose to do is their business. I try not to intrude unless I'm asked. I've brought them up, and released them, and the more you let go, the more you love them for what they are, the more they love you for letting them be what they are.

Jack Ford: "I've never been that good at keeping in touch. I think that's more my problem than anyone else's. But it's obviously more pleasant to go home now.

"I feel closer to Mother. I think, also, her recovery taught us a great lesson, that nothing is hopeless, that you can face up to whatever bad thing happens in your life. As bad as it was for the family, Mother's problem has been a hundredfold worse for her. But she's like a whole new person. She really looks forward to living each day, whatever glitches occur don't put her in a negative attitude. You know how some people sort of live from problem to problem? Instead of from good moment to good moment? To me, that's the difference in Mother now.

"I think she and I are both oversensitive. I think we can seem very smiling and open on the surface, but both of us have a tendency to keep a lot of things to ourselves. That can be agonizing, and I think it's one of the things Mother has been able to put behind her. And someday I hope I can duplicate her success in that regard."

Mike Ford: "I'm overcome by the changes in my mother. In her alcoholism, she was very self-centered, she was very, very sensitive to what you said, what you did or didn't do. For her, everything was viewed in terms of her own well-being. And she had no real interest in other people's needs. That is all changed. What has been so remarkable is that here I have a person writing letters, phoning, going out of her way to find out how we're doing. She's very attentive, very alert to what's going on in our lives. Gayle and I were talking about it, it's almost as though we are getting to know a whole new person. It's kind of like I'm getting to know my mother for the first time. I think it's a real miracle that her life has been transformed as it has.

"A while ago, she came out to Wake Forest University, where I'm on the staff, to give the Founder's Day lecture, the convocation program. She had worked very hard preparing to say something that would be from the heart and challenge the community here. There was a huge gathering, two thousand or more—students, faculty, people from the outside.

"Interestingly, there were literally hundreds of women in the audience who were looking to Mother for hope and courage. I know because of notes that were passed to me, and messages and calls that came later. Many of these women had suffered through cancer, or an alcohol-drug problem, so they came to hear her story. And I was sitting there in the front row, and she got up to speak and it was the most emotional, overwhelming experience I have had since the intervention.

"I looked up at this woman who is my mother and thought to myself that eight, ten years ago, there's no way she could have done what she was doing at that moment.

"What she was doing was in a very personal way articulating how the healing of a person involves the body, the mind and the spirit. Hers was a message of holistic healing. She related some of her own pilgrimage, her own struggles, how she had hit bottom and come face to face with death and by the grace of God had been brought back again. And that it was not only a medical or physical transformation as she got off the drugs and felt better, it was also an emotional and spiritual experience. She was able to love herself again, able to love her family again, able to experience, in a spiritual way, God's love for her and His acceptance.

"It was such a powerful message. To me, it represented the complete circle of healing. That she, sick as she had been, was now up there speaking these words of great hope and encouragement to many others who were struggling."

147

Steve Ford: "I can't imagine trying to run our family the way we used to. It would be terrible if we had to go back to the way it used to be, knowing how wonderful it is now. Because you can't have a family with one person missing. It's like you don't let one person play the game. That just doesn't work. I guess we could have kidded ourselves the rest of our lives, but something made us want to change, and it was Mother's strength that finally got us over the hump.

"She was never a bad person. She always wanted to be a good mother, but I think there were times drinking got in the way. She was not able to function sometimes as a thinking human being, and we kids took advantage of that, we learned how to get away with little things.

"Somebody asked me if I blame my father at all. I don't. When he met Mom, he was the all-American guy, college football, law school, Navy, Yale, good-looking, running for Congress, the whole shot. Who wouldn't want to be married to him? That's what dreams are made of. But Dad is one of those guys that delegate responsibility. Everybody has his responsibility, and you put your head down and get it done. He never starts a project and quits, and he expects other people to be the same way.

"After they got married, Dad expected to serve the country, and I think he expected Mom to raise his family, and it all went fine for a long, long time.

"But when Dad became a leader in the House of Representatives, and Mother started developing a problem with drinking and the prescriptions, it got real complicated. Because Dad didn't look back. He kept going. He had a job to do, and he expected her to get done whatever she was supposed to get done.

"Dad has tunnel vision, he's set in his direction, and Mother sort of got left by the wayside, not because he didn't love her, but because he didn't understand.

"He was not one to backtrack and pick up people that couldn't keep marching. He kept going, she stumbled, and the wonderful thing is that he finally came back and got her. He slowed down enough to reeducate himself, to find out what was the problem. Mom helped herself a lot, but if Dad hadn't turned around and come back and got her—

"Everybody's got a little piece in this thing, but to me, theirs is a wonderful love story."

Not only do my children like me better since my recovery; my husband and I have never been so close either. Which is a paradox, since we are so often far apart. It used to be that he was running all the time. Now we're both running. On our thirty-seventh anniversary, we had our first breakfast together in a week, and I said, "Well, maybe it's good that we just have a lot of changing scenery all the time. At least this way we don't have time for changing partners."

Jerry's an inspiration to much younger people. He can be out playing golf, come home, have dinner, fly to New York, make a speech, attend a banquet, get back on a plane and fly to Texas in time for a board meeting the next morning. (He never believed that sleep accomplished much; when I married him, he thought anything over five hours was an absolute waste of time.) Sometimes I say to him, "I can't possibly keep up with you, you ought to trade me for a newer model, honey," and he says, "I don't want a newer model, I'm happy with you." I don't know. If you turned in a sixty-eight-year-old, could you get two thirty-four-year-olds? That wouldn't be bad.

We appreciate each other more these days. I no longer resent his traveling, because he's very understanding about my traveling, and when we get home we're both ready to put our feet up; neither of us is nagging the other to go dancing. Sometimes our schedules are a joke. Once, we were both in Columbus, Ohio, on the same day, staying at different hotels, because we were on different projects. We had to phone to say how much we missed each other.

He's always called me every day from wherever he's been. He's a very thoughtful man. But as I have grown in my recovery, so has he. I've said that, in the early days, he could never tell me he loved me. He was too much the lawyer, so programmed and efficient. I had to know in my heart how much he cared, because

149

the words just weren't there. He was ambitious, he was aggressive, he wanted to be successful for his family—I still wonder sometimes if he knows he's successful—he wasn't a sweet-talker. Now it just knocks me for a loop that he's learned to express his feelings. He calls me from halfway around the world—"I had six hours' sleep, I feel pretty good, I'm getting ready to go to the board meeting, and I just want to tell you that I love you and I miss you."

Jerry Ford: "It isn't just her family that loves Betty. She's far more popular than I. Many people think she could have been elected President of the United States in 1976.

"I often acknowledge this after somebody has got up and announced me, with a lot of flowery phrases, at a banquet. I say, 'Well, I'm deeply grateful for your generous words; I need the morale boost. The reason I need it is because of an introduction a master of ceremonies made in southern California a couple of weeks ago. But before I tell you how he introduced me, let me give you a little background.'

"Then I talk about Betty's public acclaim, and I say our second son, Jack, has been a TV commentator and is a prospective politician in the San Diego area, and our third son, Steve, is a star on the daytime CBS soap opera *The Young and the Restless.* At that point, any little girls in the audience titter. Then I say, 'Well, with that background, let me tell you how this man introduced me. He got up and said, "It's my pleasure to present Betty Ford's husband, Jack Ford's dad and Steve Ford's father." So I thank you for helping my morale.'

"Seriously, Betty has always been talented. But the challenge of the Center brought out special skills that had been kind of hidden. She not only raised most of the money, but she is a hands-on chairman of the board. I tease her about it. I say I'm jealous because she spends so much time over there that I feel neglected.

"But to have seen the Center go from an idea to a successful operation gives her tremendous satisfaction, particularly to see

150

people come in very sick and leave a few weeks later totally different, healthy, vigorous, with a future ahead of them.

"Betty has changed so much. Now when she addresses an audience, she has confidence that her subject matter is of interest to them. She's more articulate, more persuasive. She was always well-intentioned, but now, whether she's talking about her individual recovery or about alcoholism, she has become a professional speaker, and everybody is impressed, including me.

"And she is a much more meaningful partner on a day-to-day basis. When I say, 'We ought to do this or this,' she wants to know why, she asks tough questions. So it's a more equal relationship than it used to be.

"Somebody asked me if I ever got tired of her talking about alcoholism. I said no, not at all. I think it's good for other people, and I think it's good for her.

"She has a big audience out there in the country. Whether I go to Tennessee, or Tallahassee, women come up and say, 'I sure wish Betty was here. Where is she?' and I have to tell them, Salt Lake, or Midland, Texas, or wherever she happens to be.

"In the course of her recovery, I've become healthier myself. I stopped drinking a year after she did. I realized I'd never really enjoyed it, it was just that I had become socially addicted.

"It was relatively simple for me to stop. I didn't want to drink alone, I wanted to lose some weight, I had no craving for liquor, and I saw how much benefit it was for her. It would be much harder for me to stop smoking a pipe."

Never mind his pipe. His real weakness is dessert. When he was trying to lose weight, he said, "I'll give up my martinis before I'll give up my ice cream." Now that's not an alcoholic speaking.

We never stopped having liquor in the house as some people do. We *did* stop having various medications in the house, because any mood-altering or addictive drug was more of a temptation to me than alcohol. If I was in a lot of pain with my neck, with my back, with arthritis, I wouldn't be apt to go take a drink. But the drugs were seductive; I knew they could give me relief, as well as the euphoric feeling that nothing mattered, that the house could burn down and it would be okay because somehow somebody would fix it.

I know pain can be emotional too, and I know a drug is a drug is a drug, and alcohol is just as mood-altering as a tranquilizer, but I was more frightened of medications, more frightened that I might use something and get hooked on it. (After I'd been sober for three years, Joe Cruse said, "Well, Betty, maybe I should bring back all those pills we cleaned out of your medicine cabinet and let you have a look at them." And I said, "Sure, Joe, bring them over." And he said, "Well, you'll have to wait a little while because there were so many I'm going to have to go over to the market and swipe a grocery cart to carry them all.")

Back when we began this book, my daughter Susan said, "You could do a whole chapter on the healing of a family," and I kept thinking about that. You hurt your family when you're sick; when you recover, so does the family. If you are lucky, their injuries mend along with yours. But not always right away. Susan, who had done so much to bring me help, was not altogether pleased by the mother who emerged from treatment.

Susan Ford: "I saw a change in her immediately, and at first, I didn't like it at all. I couldn't stand it. All of a sudden she was aware, all of a sudden it was 'Where are you going? With whom? What time are you going to be home?' And I was like, get off my back, you never paid attention before, why should you start paying attention now?

"It was like watching a brand-new rose bloom, and it was really beautiful, but it was a pain in the neck too. I had kind of done everything, and all of a sudden she was taking over the reins again.

"Now it's fine. We can be honest with each other and not hurt each other. I can tell her things I could never have told her before, and they don't bother her, she accepts them. She's interested in what I think, what everyone in the family thinks. She came to us kids when they were first talking about naming the Center, and she said, 'Do you want them to name it after me?' We said that was no problem. She said, 'Well, after I die, I want one of you always to be on the board and participate. And your children are going to grow up with a grandmother who has an alcoholics' hospital named after her. Is that going to bother you? Because if it is, I don't want it to happen.' We talked about it for a long time."

I also went to the family before I agreed to appear on all those TV shows when the Center first opened. I said, "I'm not going to do any of this if you guys don't want me to, because I don't want anybody embarrassed." The children said they were proud of what I was doing. "We've got you back healthy, and if it's going to help other people, and you want to do it, you should be able to do it."

Looking back now, I don't think my husband or the boys ever had the resentments Susan had. She was the one who rescued me, but she was also the one who most felt the hurt of my illness. Always. Beginning when she was little and didn't know what was wrong with me because I was so emotionally drained and upset. She didn't think I was alcoholic then, she thought I was crazy, and she didn't want a crazy mother.

After she married, she and Chuck moved to Huntington Beach, just a couple of blocks away from Pat Benedict, and she had a lot of help from Pat in working through her problems with —and about—me.

Meri Bell once told me she'd gone to a meeting of a support group for families of alcoholics. "And all I could think," she said, "was what damn fools they are. They put up with stuff from their alcoholics that I would never have put up with from anybody." Still, she said, "you can't go on manipulating your family forever. Eventually your kids know you are conning them. Other people know it too, but your kids have to live with it, whereas the other people can walk away."

Well, I did manipulate my family, but I didn't know any other way—if I didn't want to do something, I traded on their love or their sympathy to get me out of doing it. And then I think Susan just got fed up. The family of an alcoholic *has* to get fed up.

It took time for me to accept that I had taken advantage of

my family. After all, I reasoned, nobody else was affected by my alcoholism or drug dependency, it was just something I did to myself. In those early days of recovery, I knew meetings with other recovering alcoholics were important. I made myself attend them, and gradually, I began to hear a little, and understand a little. Still, when I listened to people talking about being hurt or angry or resentful or guilty, I was confused, because I really couldn't feel much. I didn't know what feeling was, I hadn't done it in a long time.

Since I've been active in the field of treatment, I've learned how even little children—six, seven, eight years old—are affected by the alcoholism of their parents. They are ashamed and guilty, they wonder what they did to make their parents drink. There's a lot of agony in that. If we can get a child into treatment at the same time that his mother or father is being treated, we can help him begin to understand it's a disease, and it isn't his fault. In Al-Anon, children are told that, eventually, they will have to learn to ignore the alcoholic and go about their own lives. It's a hard lesson.

For anybody, not just children. We knew people, a very proper churchgoing couple, and she was a periodic drinker. If they had an important social engagement, he would telephone one of her friends and say, "I want to pick up R. at five o'clock. We have to go to a reception and dinner. Will you stay with her till then?" The friend would have to spend the day, make sure R. didn't start drinking, so she would be in shape for the evening's business. And if R. was home alone, and got herself absolutely blotto, passed out on the floor, her husband had learned to deal with that too. He'd come in, take one look and step over her, go watch the news, get up, go out, get some dinner and come home again. By then, maybe she'd picked herself up and crawled into bed. You should not be responsible for the mess an alcoholic makes of his or her life.

When I came home from Long Beach, my family—except, maybe briefly, for Susan—was ecstatic because in their minds everything was okay again. They had all been to Long Beach themselves for bits and pieces of treatment, but not through a

154

real family program. At Long Beach, wives, husbands, children of alcoholics were in therapy right along with their alcoholics, rather than in separate groups.

At the Betty Ford Center, family members are regarded as patients. You don't get to just sit around and bitch about what it's like at home, and what a dirty deal you got having to live with that creature all these years. You have to talk about yourself, and why you feel the way you feel, and sometimes it sort of comes out that maybe you are not perfect either.

Alcoholism is a family disease. We tell this to our inpatients, and we tell it to their parents and their children and their mates. We would tell it to their uncles and their cousins and their aunts, if those relations came around. It's important for everyone to know the extent to which the disease affects all those around it.

During the four to six weeks that a patient is in treatment at the Center, we ask family members to spend five days there too. Sometimes, they don't want to. One of them will say to the counselor who has contacted him, "Why should I come? *I* don't have the problem."

They're right. They have a different problem. Family members are in denial. They don't communicate with each other or the patient. And they don't know they're sick. But enabling is a sickness. An enabler's addiction is to the alcoholic. And usually, everyone in a family is required to be an enabler, to cover up, to mop up. Your twenty-year-old son is arrested? You pay the fine. Your husband is drunk? You don't go out to dinner.

That's the sickness, that's the family disease of alcoholism. It's as if your hands are tied, you don't know what to do, and you're scared to do anything, and you hope if you don't do anything, maybe it'll all go away, clear itself up.

"Alcoholism is like having an elephant in the living room, and we don't talk about it," is the way one of the counselors at the Center describes the denial.

Why don't we talk about it? That's easy. We're quick learners. We know that if you confront the alcoholic, you get back so much rage it isn't worth the effort.

Enablers, co-dependents, whatever you want to call those

who live with chemically addicted people, have to step back and look at the disease, and realize they didn't cause it, they can't control it, and they can't cure it.

We tell the people who come to family treatment that they *must* let go. But it can be hard to let go, because the person who cares for and takes care of the sick person is also sick in his or her own way.

In five days of therapy, family members are not going to get as heavy a program as the inpatient does, but what they do get gives them a handle on their situation. And that's what they're asked to concentrate on, *their* program. They're not even allowed to spend time with the inpatient. They can wave when they pass on the campus, and they're welcome at certain lectures, and they see the same movies the patients see, but they're all supposed to be working out their new lives separately.

For the alcoholic, the first step is to admit you're powerless over alcohol and other mood-altering chemicals, and your life has become unmanageable. For the family member, the first step is to recognize, and accept *on a feeling level,* your powerlessness over addiction, dependency and an addicted, dependent person.

In the family program at the Center, the family member is forced to face his preoccupation with the chemically dependent person, the devices he's been using to try to punish the chemically dependent person—insults, silent treatment, laying on guilt —along with covering up the problem, enabling.

Some enablers are drama junkies, and when the alcoholic starts to get well, the excitement goes out of their days. They have to face this; there are people who do not want the sick person to get better.

Many women who divorce alcoholics turn right around and marry other alcoholics. They're attracted to people they think need help.

And then the children come along, and they are affected. They are embarrassed, and don't want to bring their friends home after school. They are confused, because one minute Mommy is throwing out Daddy's bottles and haranguing him,

156

and the next minute she's calling his office to say he can't come to work; he has a cold or the flu or a toothache.

Kids see all this convoluted love-hate, and they get into the act too. The children of alcoholics play many parts. Quite often, the first-born plays the hero, is a good student, takes over, tries to help fix the damage. Then there's the scapegoat, who misbehaves to get attention (he's the one who may end up in trouble with the police; he's defiant, withdrawn, the most apt to use drugs, the most apt to commit suicide). Then there's the mascot, who tends to be hyperactive, clowns, tries to distract the family from its troubles (and covers up his own feelings), and there's the lost child, who hides out in his room.

These are all survival roles, and all of these children are preoccupied with the alcoholic. The alcoholic is running things, pushing everybody's buttons, watching them react, keeping the family off balance, making them bounce around trying to compensate for the disruption.

Dr. Pursch always felt if you could get the rest of the family into treatment, even when the patient would *not* go for help, you could do some good. When you teach a family to walk away, and not to let the alcoholic upset them, you reach the alcoholic too. Because once he is no longer the center of everyone's attention, he says, hey, what's going on here? He can't push their buttons anymore.

Family treatment is similar in many ways to the in-patient program. The family members struggle in group to find their identities and to learn how best to survive their co-dependency.

To give you an idea of the exchange of feelings that goes on in a family program, let me suggest a hypothetical group made up of composites of patients I have known during my eight years of sobriety:

Patient One: A woman still angry about an accident she's had eight years before (her husband, off drinking, was not with her when she drove herself to the hospital).

Patient Two: A woman whose addict son blames her for his father's desertion of the family.

Patient Three: A young rock musician whose father is an in-

157

patient, but who realizes he has a drug problem of his own. "In the end, I can't blame my pot on anyone else," he says. "It's my ass, nobody else's."

Patient Four: A middle-aged gentleman who is horrified by some of the language he hears in group. He has come to family—his son is a drug addict—and has grown fond of his fellow patients, but the vernacular of the young ones still shocks him. When a girl stands up one day and says, "Well, I think it's important to call a spade a spade," the middle-aged gentleman just shakes his head. "In this group," he says, "they don't call a spade a spade, they call it a f—ing shovel." Then he blushes.

Out of such disparate groups comes the same kind of bonding we find with the inpatients, and it's even more mysterious since these people aren't together twenty-four hours a day. At the Betty Ford Center, family is a more or less nine to five business, the sessions start after breakfast and end before dinner. The program is intensive—films, lectures, group therapy—and if you want to come back after dinner, there are meetings and Al-Anon meetings. Local participants commute from home, while most of the out-of-towners stay at a nearby motel which provides bus service back and forth.

With family members, the same as with inpatients, much of the learning process goes on during breaks. People gather in the lounge, where there are soft drinks, coffee, fruit and cake. The fat ones eat pastries, and the skinny ones smoke, and everyone exchanges stories and discovers he or she is not so different, so alien.

What the counselors try to do is teach the families to love the alcoholic, not his behavior. Recently, a woman came, reluctantly, to family. Six months earlier, her husband had been through treatment, but in spite of his present sobriety, she was still very angry.

"He wasn't the sweet old man you see here, when he was drinking," she said. "And if he was breathing, he was drinking. I had ten terrible years because of it.

"I was so mad. My husband never understood why. 'What do you want?' he would say. 'Why don't you go buy yourself a fur coat?'

"I don't understand this program. Nothing happened until I told my husband, 'I'm through.' Then he came and got help."

It was pointed out to this woman that when she had said she was through, she had stopped enabling, and this surprised her. She had never heard the word before. At the time her husband had come for treatment, she had refused to go through family. "I've put up with his drinking all these years," she said. "There's no reason I should go and find out it's my fault, or something."

By the time she went home, she had changed. "I found out I didn't have to be the general," she said. "I found out I was not alone."

Sometimes there is so much bitterness or lack of interest that out of six family members, only one is willing to show up and be counted. We had a pilot who had almost no support (his wife had divorced him), but his little boy came to treatment. He was only six or eight years old, and I remember his drawings of all kinds of airplanes, because planes were a big thing in his father's life.

There's plenty of black humor in family too. One mother and father whose son was in North Hall said, "We gave him a gift certificate to Betty Ford for Christmas."

People who have never confided in anyone at all suddenly break through in family therapy sessions, pouring out the pent-up sickness of years. "I hate my husband, he's a drunk, he doesn't give me any money, he says I'm a mess, my clothes aren't coordinated right, I'm a joke. And I'm angry at my daughter because she joined a religious cult, and now my darling little grandsons aren't allowed to celebrate Christmas."

In treatment, people stop intellectualizing, stop rationalizing, and start feeling. They start to see that if your alcoholic totals the car, you shouldn't be saying it wasn't his fault, there was a tree in the middle of the road.

Co-alcoholics lie to themselves a hundred ways. One of our counselors invents an example. "My uncle's alcoholic. He has a tattoo and is in the Navy, so everyone who's alcoholic must have tattoos and be in the Navy. My aunt was not alcoholic because she didn't have tattoos, and she wasn't in the Navy. She died at forty-two of cirrhosis of the liver, but—"

159

Most family members who come to us believe they are here to support the alcoholic. We emphasize that they are here for themselves.

Another counselor who has worked very effectively with children says that the first question kids ask her is how they can get a parent to stop using. They're guilty, they think it's their fault. Older children suffer guilt when they feel they have abandoned an alcoholic parent. "I couldn't stand to see him like that, so I'd leave. I'd say I had a date, even if I just had a date with my dog," one boy said, breaking down in group because his father had died and it was too late to fix anything anymore.

We families who get help in time to fix things are the ones who have been blessed.

I remember Mike and Gayle at my intervention saying they wanted a healthy grandmother for their children. I had no grandchildren then, I have five now. Susan and Chuck have two little girls, Mike and Gayle have three. I went back East for Hannah Gayle's christening in February 1986, and Jerry and I spent a couple of days with Mike, Gayle, Sarah, Rebekah and the new baby. And I got to put six-year-old Sarah to bed. She is accustomed to being tucked in with a song and a prayer, so after I sang "Jesus Loves Me," she said, "What about the prayer?"

"Well," I said, "I usually say the Lord's Prayer. Let me teach you that one." And I got as far as "forgive us our trespasses," and she said, "Gramma, what's a trespass?" Time out. Ten minutes while I'm trying to figure how to explain to a six-year-old what a trespass is. "It's like when you're mean to one of your friends or classmates, and hurt their feelings," I said. "Because then you hurt God's feelings."

Three weeks later, I was talking to Mike on the phone, and I could hear Sarah yelling something in the background. He said what she was yelling was "You gotta tell Gramma I've put all the information about trespassing on my tape recorder."

Sarah is not going to hurt God's feelings if she can possibly avoid it.

With Susan's children too, I relish being "Gramma." I was in Virginia in February 1983, right after Heather, the second Vance

160

baby, was born. Chuck was away on a trip, and there was a storm. It turned into a real blizzard, and we were snowed in. I couldn't get back home—where I had a speaking engagement—because the Washington airport was closed.

It was a wonderful adventure. We had to have wood brought in to keep the fires going, and it was so cold Susan and I ended up sleeping together. There were three generations of us, mother, daughter, granddaughters, in the house. I took snapshots of Tyne, who's three years older than Heather, lying on the floor coloring with crayons, and she went out with me to shop at the supermarket, and I cooked. I made meat loaf and pot roast and roasted chicken. I was the mother taking care of her child again, this child who had so courageously taken care of me. And here was this new baby who was such a wonder. Susan and I were happy, sharing so much love and gratitude. I think we were realizing the circle of life.

The healing of a family, Susan had called it. It can be a chain reaction. Wellness spreading from one to another. And you don't need to have gone through the family program at the Betty Ford Center to get there either; there are many roads back to sanity, and sometimes one person's resolution to be healthy again is enough to carry a whole crowd along. Mike and Gayle got a firsthand example of what I'm talking about when they visited the Center in March 1985.

Mike Ford: "Gayle and I went West to a conference, and spent the night with the folks, and then, on a Saturday morning, Mom took us over to the Betty Ford Center. We had missed the Dedication—it came at a time when we couldn't get away—so this was the first time we had been there.

"We walked all through this wonderful facility, saw the rooms, met the staff and some patients, came out again and were about to get into the car when these two kids rode right up in front of the Center on their ten-speed bikes.

"It turned out they were on spring break from San Diego State and they'd backpacked their way across all those miles. They were wearing cutoffs, and they were all sunburned and windblown from the long trip. It was a pilgrimage of sorts for them. They were coming to the place where their father had found recovery, and they just wanted to go in and see it and experience it for themselves.

"They were brother and sister, their father was an alcoholic, and in fact the sister was an alcoholic too, and they had had terrible domestic problems at home. They weren't expecting to see Mother, but they rushed right over to her and introduced themselves, and the words of gratitude poured out.

" 'We just need to tell you what you and this place have meant in the lives of our family,' the boy said, and the girl broke in: 'We have gone through hell. My father came here as a last resort, he went through eight weeks of therapy, and he's now been sober for a year. He came back and helped me get into AA, and there's been so much reconciliation and healing in our home because of this experience we just have to tell you how grateful we are and how much we love you.'

"Gayle and I were standing back watching and listening in amazement, and these kids were crying. I got all choked up, and Mother didn't know what to say. But to me that scene represented the feelings of a lot of people who have been touched by Mom's experiences, and by the Center. It was both a thrilling and enlightening moment for me."

13

O Rose, thou art sick!
The invisible worm
That flies in the night,
In the howling storm,

Has found out thy bed
Of crimson joy,
And his dark secret love
Does thy life destroy.

William Blake

Like the invisible worm that eats at the heart of the rose, drugs and alcohol are dark secret lovers that destroy. I have heard those patients who say, "Cocaine loves me." It wasn't until 1955 that the American Medical Association finally said—out loud, and in print—"Alcoholism is a disease." Not that this was accepted with wild acclaim by the entire medical establishment.

But I don't want all the doctors in the United States mad at me, so let me add that society in general is even less swift than its doctors to recognize that sick people are not just out there making trouble.

Joe Cruse wrote a fascinating parable called "When the Stigma Is Gone." Here it is, somewhat abridged:

"She had been concerned about him for a long time. He was acting differently, he was missing more work, he had lost his vigor, he was quick to snap at the kids, and most distasteful, in bed at night he would sweat profusely, waking her with his mumbling and restlessness. Next day, he would have no recollection. On occasion she sent him to their dear friend and physician, who backed up his allegation that 'he had the flu again.'

"On one occasion, she confronted him with her diagnosis and he exploded and hit her, for the first time in their marriage.

"Their daughter was engaged to the son of a very prominent family, and it was a foregone conclusion that if the future in-laws became aware of his disease, there would be no marriage.

"He couldn't face the thought that he might have that disease. People who had it lost jobs, families, had to be sent away to one of those places for 'the cure,' and there were no funds or insurance to pay for it.

"His boss had approached him and said he was concerned about his absenteeism, decreasing job performance and increasing inability to get along with his fellow workers.

"He considered moving to another state. When he was particularly bothered, he would isolate himself, and only return when he had control, but still appearing much the worse for wear. Then one morning the bed was full of blood. His wife immediately took him to the physician, who finally had to tell him that, in this new year of 1911, he was suffering from advanced tuberculosis."

Isn't that amazing? The physical symptoms, the social stigma, the doctor's unwillingness to tell the truth—but Joe is talking about tuberculosis, not alcoholism. Where tuberculosis was in 1911, alcoholism was in the thirties, the forties, the fifties. And still is today in some places.

It was in that year, 1911, that Dr. William Oursler wrote that as long as science looked upon the spread of TB as "a behavioral problem," it held out "small hope of recovery to the stricken one."

In the matter of alcoholism, not only has science looked upon drinking as "a behavioral problem," some doctors have not cared to look upon it at all.

Shortly before Christmas of 1985, the New York *Times* ran an

164

article headlined "Doctors Learning to Diagnose Alcoholism." In it, journalist Nadine Brozan wrote of a depressed college dropout who went to see a psychiatrist. The psychiatrist said the girl was suffering because she had been small as a child. "I told him I was drinking and taking drugs—marijuana, LSD—but he didn't want to discuss that at all," the onetime student informed Ms. Brozan.

A year later, the same girl went to another psychiatrist, and he announced that she was simply going through an identity crisis. And "although she candidly described her dependence on alcohol and drugs," reported Ms. Brozan, "the doctor dismissed it."

So did several other doctors. "Six more years elapsed, and finally a psychiatrist—whose name she had found in the Yellow Pages—said, 'Do you have a problem with alcohol?' and referred her to Alcoholics Anonymous." Where she found her sobriety.

But Ms. Brozan, who interviewed a good many doctors in the course of her research, wrote, "The stone wall this patient encountered is not unusual."

Too many psychiatrists and other physicians contribute to addiction and help maintain addicts in their habits. Because while they don't dispense alcohol, they do write prescriptions. Mostly for women. And women, more than men, become dependent on their doctors and on the drugs they prescribe. A woman thinks her doctor can help her emotionally as well as physically. And we love those prescriptions. We've spent a long time waiting for the appointment, we've got dressed and gone to the office, we're going to have a hefty bill to pay, and we don't want to go home without that little white piece of paper covered in hen tracks; it's the return on our investment of time and money.

Let me recap my own medical history. As a young housewife in Washington, D.C., I began taking daily medication for a pinched nerve in my neck. The pills eased my pain as I chased four active little children.

My children grew, and so did my pill habit. Then came pancreatitis, tactfully shrugged off as a gallbladder or stomach disorder. In all my years in Washington, no doctor ever specifically made a reference to my misuse or abuse of alcohol. And I never made any connection between drinking and a health problem.

I now believe some doctors choose to be uninformed about chemical dependency and to ignore the impact of combining alcohol with pills.

I had a gourmet collection of drugs—I did a little self-prescribing; if one pill is good, two must be better—and when I added vodka to the mix, I moved into a wonderful fuzzy place where everything was fine, I could cope.

If, as Dolores Hope says, my friends were talking about my "problem," and noticing that my health was deteriorating, I still did not blame myself, disavowing all responsibility. For years, doctors had been giving me pills, and I had never questioned them. In my early recovery, I was angry with all of them. But as I grew in recovery, and began more fully to understand my disease, I realized I was responsible, it was my body that was being assaulted, I was the one who was feeding it pills and drinks. I could have asked questions about what I was taking, but I didn't. The fuzzy feeling was too nice.

There was enough blame for all of us, the doctors and me. They were of a generation faced with a proliferation of new, mood-altering, miracle drugs. They hadn't been taught about alcoholism and addiction, and even when they recognized the symptoms, they turned away. Addiction was just too messy to try and treat.

Often, these doctors were angry with patients who had so little "willpower," and many of them were still committed to the hypocrisy of the double standard—women couldn't be alcoholic, and certainly the wife of a former President couldn't be involved in anything so disgusting.

It was a generation of doctors who felt it was easier to write a prescription for a woman than to listen to her complaints and try to find her real problem. Diagnosis on a more serious level could take hours. And women were neurotic little things, and the waiting room was full of patients.

Today, things aren't quite as bad as they were a few years ago, because more women are going into medicine, because through television and newspapers and magazines, the public is learning more about the epidemic of chemical dependency which has swept the country, and because some medical schools —Dartmouth and Johns Hopkins, to name a couple—have begun to concentrate on alcohol education.

But it still is not enough. More medical schools have to offer more courses, require more study, and teach what is now learned for the most part only by accident and through intuition.

Joe Cruse is a recovering alcoholic. So is Jim West, who became medical director of the Betty Ford Center when Joe decamped for a job with another treatment center. We regretted his leaving, but Joe is a visionary, he is always searching for the next challenge. Without him, the Betty Ford Center might not have happened.

The personal experience and empathy brought to us by Joe Cruse and Jim West were invaluable, but it's my view that *all* doctors ought to be trained to recognize alcoholism, even if they themselves have never hoisted a glass.

Jim West: "I am a surgeon by specialty, but back in the seventies I also taught substance abuse in the Department of Psychiatry at the University of Chicago. At that time, very little was known in the medical profession about alcoholism and drug dependence.

"Alcoholism and education about it has been kind of a confusing issue to the medical community. They're not for it or against it, they just don't understand it.

"In 1975, because I recognized what chemical dependency had done to me (I stopped drinking in 1958), I started a Program for the Impaired Physician for the Illinois State Medical Society. We trained medical staff, informed them as to what chemical dependency was and also drove home a message: If you cover up for an impaired physician who is functioning poorly, you are helping him to commit suicide. If you love your brother physician, you must get him help. This kind of led the way for doctors to intervene on other doctors. More importantly, perhaps, this program served to protect patients of impaired physicians.

167

"At the Betty Ford Center, I give the patients three lectures; they are a condensation of the best lectures I gave to my medical students, because I think alcoholics are so smart there is little they can't understand.

"Our treatment here is eclectic; we've taken the best techniques from everywhere and incorporated all the things that have been learned about chemical dependency that work. I think everybody who works here likes working here, and this enjoyment spills over onto the patient. There is a special feeling between the staff and patients that may also exist in other good programs but doesn't exist in other aspects of medicine. (As a surgeon, whether or not I liked the patient had nothing to do with my effectiveness.)

"We treat everyone the same. Superstar types adjust in about one half hour, because if they look at themselves as too special to follow our program, we will help them find another place, but we will not adjust to them.

"The bonding that goes on here is magic, indescribable. Having said that, I will now try to describe it. In psychiatric terms, we have people in extreme distress, they are terribly vulnerable, their defenses are dropping away, their ego boundaries are gone, it's like they are falling in love with everybody.

"Those defenses were the only things left in their survival kit. We've already taken away their drugs. The idea is, we trust the person but we don't trust the illness.

"For me, this place is a tremendous gift. I was blessed in my sobriety to do this work I love. I am seventy-two years old, and if it weren't for the BFC, I would probably look and act like eighty-two, instead of feeling like forty-one."

There is a full-time medical department at the Center; Jim West has three other doctors to assist him in giving physical exams. But Jim is as good a teacher as he is a doctor. He never talks down to patients. He *does* believe alcoholics are smart enough to understand whatever he says, no matter how technical it gets. I like to hear him lecture. He says he spent most of his life in green pajamas and a surgical mask—"I was a repairman"—and he's still repairing people.

He tells patients, "This disease is chronic, and this disease is primary. It isn't that people have something *else* the matter with them, and that's what makes them drink; it's that they have a psychological lesion—we think the site is in the brain—and it's genetically transmissible."

He says that every recovering alcoholic must always be aware of the possibility of a relapse into drinking, because our personality traits are like "a snake who lies back in a dark corner of the mind and who, every now and then, maybe every three or four years, will open one eye to see if the alcoholic is still on guard."

Every patient who comes to the Center gets a physical examination and a psychological evaluation, along with a chest X ray and a full spectrum of laboratory tests.

In time, we want to reserve a couple of beds in each of our residence halls for medical students, and maybe administrators of other hospitals, and nurses, have them actually go through the treatment process as part of their education. We're just going to have to feel our way along in this, but we know the need is great.

Over and over, we see the evidence. When I was in Long Beach, the Navy had made it mandatory for all Navy doctors to go through treatment, so they'd recognize the disease when they came up against it. Well, out of every group that went in for training, a couple of people discovered that they themselves were alcoholics, and elected to stay on as patients. I think they would have been reluctant to seek treatment on their own. Just as in their professional lives, they were reluctant to diagnose and refer to treatment other alcoholics and addicts.

Jim West: "Recent research *(Alcoholism: An Inherited Disease—NIAAA)* makes it increasingly clear that heredity is a major contributing cause of alcoholism. Findings in these studies lead to the conclusion that there are two kinds of genetic predisposition to this disease. One is termed Milieu-limited Alcoholism and the other is called Male-limited.

"Milieu-limited Alcoholism is the most common form of this illness. It effects both men and women and its severity is thought to be determined by environmental factors in genetically susceptible persons.

"Male-limited Alcoholism is a much more severe type of the disease, transmitted by the alcoholic father to the son. It is not influenced by environment and frequently develops in adolescence. It is thought that about 25 percent of male alcoholics fall into this category. Male-limited susceptibility in a family does not increase the risk of alcohol abuse in daughters.

"There are promising studies which may one day identify neurophysiological and enzyme markers to help us understand the genetics of alcoholism and help us design strategies for prevention in susceptible persons."

Eternal vigilance is the price of sobriety.

Alcoholics can't drink. It would be nice if they could, but they can't. Except in the fantasy worlds of the certain mistaken "experts."

I have nothing against fantasy. If Jerry comes into the study and says, "It's doubtful that your son is going to survive. He was shot twice in the abdomen, and he's losing blood," we can laugh, because Steve's wounds were actually inflicted on the character of Andy Richards during the course of *The Young and the Restless,* and the blood is fake.

But doctors and other scientists who have tested their theories of "controlled" drinking on alcoholics have failed miserably to prove their points. And too many of the alcoholics who tried to drink again, died. It wasn't a soap opera where, after the lights faded, the murdered actors got up and went home.

Still, the medical profession can't be blamed for all the woes of the alcoholic.

I myself have had too much help from doctors—Dan Anderson, Joe Cruse, Stan Gitlow, Vern Johnson, Joe Pursch, Max Schneider, when we were getting the Center started—to be churlish about the profession. I've leaned on doctors, and so has my family.

170

Steve Ford: "You know, at Long Beach, the one thing I really put my faith in was the doctors and the staff around Mom, because I wasn't sure medically how serious her problem was, and what she had to do to lick it."

None of us was sure how serious my problem was, nobody knew what I had to do to lick it, but Steve's faith was not misplaced. And since my recovery, I've encountered many other fine doctors who are helping men and women to live drug-free. I just think there are still plenty of them who need to learn more.

In November 1985, I offered this opinion to a whole auditorium full of doctors. We were all attending a conference at the Annenberg Center at Eisenhower, a conference labeled "Alcohol, Drugs, and Primary Care Physician Education."

I was asked to speak, and I did. I told the history of my disease and my experiences with doctors. I closed by saying, "A doctor's ability and willingness to recognize the symptoms of alcoholism or drug dependency, to make the diagnosis and then offer viable recommendations for treatment can save lives!" And they listened. That's what I call progress.

14

A change of love: if love is a
 groping Godward, though blind,
No matter what crevice, creek, chink,
 bright in dark, the pale tentacle find.

Robert Penn Warren

Before we abandon the subject of the medical profession, did you
know that alcoholism is an equal-opportunity disease? And that
doctors, lawyers and clergymen have just as many problems with
alcohol and drug dependency as anyone else? They're all in care-
taking professions, they're trying to save other people, and they
experience a lot of stress.

Some of them work too hard, put in terrible hours, are falli-
ble human beings to whom we attribute supernatural powers. We
lean on them, demanding what they can't give. But who's taking
care of the caretakers? And why don't they lean on God? For
some reason, this is a subject that makes many modern people
uncomfortable.

It's relatively safe, unemotional, to discuss the addict's physi-
ology—lesions in the brain, genetic aberrations—but you can't
treat the flesh without taking into account the spirit. Which, sick
itself, is often unwilling to be taken into account. Many addicts
view the chemical as God. They don't need other help, except
from the bartender or the pusher or the doctor.

Ralph Waite, the actor, and a recovering alcoholic, tells a story that makes this point. It seems there was a man up in Alaska who ran into a priest. For all I know, the encounter took place in a bar. Anyway, the man walked up to the priest and said, "Father, I hate to tell you, but I've lost my faith in God and the power of prayer."

"Why is that, my son?" the priest asked politely.

The man explained. A couple of months earlier, he had been hunting in the Alaskan wilderness, and he had become separated from his friends. It was terrible, all alone out there. "I was in danger of freezing to death. So I prayed and I prayed to the Lord to save me, but nothing happened."

The priest was perplexed. "But you're here telling me your story, so obviously you were rescued."

"Oh, yes," the man said, "I was rescued, but the Lord had nothing to do with it. I was saved by an Eskimo."

Millions of us are saved by Eskimos, and don't see the hand of God in it.

This doesn't mean I don't believe we should take all the earthly help we can get. Some people may have found recovery in a church, a synagogue or a mosque, but alcoholism is a disease like cancer and arthritis, and I'm not sure praying more would have helped me avoid any of them. (Jack Benny once made a speech after having been given an award. "I don't deserve this award," he said. "But then, I've got arthritis, and I don't deserve that either.") Still, I believe that even if praying doesn't prevent our afflictions, it helps us get through them.

Meri Bell says God is very tough with us. "He gave us free will, and then sat back and watched what we did with it. A lot of times, we destroyed ourselves, and He stood by and let us. But if we turned around and said, 'Hey, will You help me?' He was there."

I've had personal experience of this. When I was hospitalized for my mastectomy, I thought, this could be it, and only God can help me. Through prayer, I let go and turned it over. This was before I knew I was alcoholic, before I had ever heard these phrases. Tension dissolved, my mind and my whole body relaxed, it was as though a huge weight had been lifted from me, as though a light had gone on. God was in my life, He would take care of me, and I was going to be all right. That day, my faith in God was reaffirmed in such a strong way that it has never really faltered since.

For me, the acceptance of a Higher Power was easier than it is for many alcoholics. Religion had always been part of my life. For the people who come into treatment wanting no part of God, it can be harder. Because almost all treatment programs are based on the twelve steps of Alcoholics Anonymous, which has a spiritual foundation. Step One simply requires us to admit we were powerless over alcohol, Step Two says we "came to believe that a Power greater than ourselves could restore us to sanity," and the third step says we "made a decision to turn our will and our lives over to the care of God *as we understood Him.*"

In a world that glorifies science and provable fact, these steps can be stumbling blocks for atheists and agnostics, even though the phrase "as we understood him" offers a lot of leeway. As one of the books published by AA says, "Some of us *won't* believe in God, others can't, and still others who do believe that God exists have no faith whatever He will perform this miracle." (The miracle of removing our obsession and giving us sobriety.)

Patients can accept that they wouldn't be in treatment if they could have got well on their own, that they need help. And they're able to ask for help from the staff of a treatment center, so they've already begun to turn their lives and wills over to something or somebody outside themselves. But for many, it's a giant leap from counselor to God.

Still, "God as you understood Him" is a phrase with wide latitude. It means you can choose as your Higher Power whatever gives you comfort, the mountains, a river, a rock, even your therapy group, the consensus of the group. The journey is spiritual, no matter what road you travel. Muriel Zink, for example, is going to Russia with a group of recovering alcoholics, and they plan to hold meetings there to share their recovery.

Muriel Zink: "We are going with sanction by the Ministry of Health, and we have to be very careful, because we are not there to proselytize, we are not there to say, 'This is the catechism, and this is the way you should do it,' we are there to share something that happened to us.

"Treatment is adaptable. The American Indians, for instance, use the concept of the Great Spirit, and they have a beautiful program that they have evolved to fit their needs.

"I think in Russia we can make the term Higher Power understandable by explaining it's like the good conscience of the collective. What I want to get across is that alcoholism is a disease and we didn't know we had it, until it almost did us in and we can share our experience in recovery and our strength and hope with you. It doesn't matter that you're Russian, and I'm a Scotch-Irish American, what matters is that I'm an alcoholic, and I have been lost."

My guide, Meri Bell, also speaks of having been lost, not because God failed her, but because she thought, in her drinking, she had failed God.

Meri Bell Sharbutt: "You see, the spiritual goes first. You go away from God because you think you shouldn't have a hangover, or you shouldn't have behaved badly; it was because you got drunk. And gradually, you stay away from church, you stay away from prayer, or you continue to go through the motions, but there is this vague unrest inside that says something is missing, something is going away.

"Alcoholism is a baffling disease, it turns you into somebody you don't know. One of the spiritual gains in recovery is that women begin to share more with other women, and that increases our courage. I have a feeling that most women isolate themselves from each other as they begin to develop façades, and that changes when they suffer enough pain to break down those defenses, those walls. You look at another woman and you find out you've been denying your own sex.

"I used to think I was a man's woman. I didn't like women. I

176

didn't trust women. That was a lie. I was the woman I didn't trust. Women alcoholics become friends as Betty and I have become friends. We don't make demands of each other, we accept each other where we are in today's pattern, knowing each of us has so much to learn, and so much to find out.

"I lost my way a long time ago. We lose our way by not maturing. We have a lot of fun and a lot of pleasure, and then we have a lot of pain and a lot of shame. We have a lot of pain getting sober. We have a lot of mental attitudes to change. We have the physical recovery. And then we begin to recover the laughter and the joy and the pleasure of not having to pretend anymore. And then we begin to find our souls."

We journey blind on our way back to family, to faith, to God, as we understand Him. But the blindness is a requisite part of the process. We can no longer control, we have to trust.

Not necessarily in any formal religion, but in a spiritual program. The people who started AA knew this. Bill Wilson, a co-founder, stubbed his toe on dogma when he first tried to get sober. He had stayed at Carl Jung's sanitarium abroad for a solid year, and two weeks after he left, he was drunk again. He came back to Jung, who said, "I think you're hopeless. Unless you have some kind of spiritual conversion, you are doomed to die."

Bill went home, joined the New York-based Oxford Group, which practiced what they called "aggressive evangelism," found the emphasis on religion too oppressive, and drank again.

In 1940, after AA was established, Bill explained why he had left the Oxford Group. He found their appetite for personal publicity dangerous to recovering alcoholics, and while he admired their "Four Absolutes—absolute honesty, purity, unselfishness and love," he believed more tolerance had to be emphasized. "We can never say to anyone (or insinuate)," he wrote, "that he must agree to our formula or be excommunicated. The atheist may stand up in an AA meeting denying God, yet reporting how he has been helped in other ways."

There are people at the Betty Ford Center who say they don't get the spiritual part of the program, and I'm sure there are

177

people at AA who say the same thing, but it does unfold gradually, as our own cobwebs lift. It's very hard to tell even ourselves, let alone God, the wrongs we have done. It's very hard to make the appropriate amends to those we have harmed. You have to be careful not to inflict more pain while you're trying to fix something. You shouldn't say, "Since I'm supposed to make amends, I better tell you I slept with your boyfriend a couple of times while you were out of town. I'm really sorry about it and I won't do it again."

I kept trying to make amends to my family by saying I didn't understand how a person as intelligent as I could be such a total failure and a mess, do this to them, embarrass them this way. The emphasis was still on me and what I had done wrong.

I had to learn to forgive myself if I expected them to forgive me. And I couldn't forgive myself until I could believe God had forgiven me.

The Lord's Prayer says, "Forgive us our trespasses, as we forgive those who trespass against us." That was the beginning.

But it was still hard to let go of the controls, to work the program of "Thy will, not my will." I also had trouble with a prayer that says you must be willing for God to have all of you, good and bad. When I first heard that, I was *not* willing. Give myself to a power greater than I, sure. But why the bad part? It was hard for me to think that the bad part of myself would be acceptable, that God didn't expect me to be perfect, or to walk on water.

I have had so much to learn. And many people have helped me learn it. Everyone fails from time to time, but in my case, it isn't for lack of trying. My understanding is that God wants me to look at facts straight, to be honest, to abide by my convictions without imposing them on anybody else.

For a long time, I couldn't look at anything straight. I was so self-blaming, I was so disappointed at what I had done to myself, my family, my body, my mind, at the way I had emptied myself, spiritually, emotionally. I had always maintained a dependence on God, but I had expected God to do everything for me.

In my early recovery, I heard Joe Cruse talking about himself, saying, "I had to finally realize that I couldn't allow my eyes just to focus inward on my problems. It was time for me to turn my eyes outward, and see other people."

That's a lesson in recovery that anyone can understand. When you find you're feeling sorry for yourself, it's time to get busy and start helping somebody else. Soon, your self-pity and self-centeredness disappear, and you feel healthier. I know it works for me.

Though there are traps in that direction too. You can't save the world. I have on occasion become too involved in counseling someone, only to find that person was not ready. I finally had to free myself of my involvement with one friend. Tell her I loved her, but I couldn't fix her, and if she wanted to drink, she must go ahead and drink. I cannot turn anyone else into a recovered person. All I can do is share my own experience, and if someone wants to make use of it, that's fine.

Recovery can't be easily defined. Certainly, there is no recovery without abstinence. You have to stop drinking and using before you can start trying to get on with your life in a constructive way. It's later that the spiritual growth begins, and it comes along slowly. You turn it over. You find out that you are not the greatest power, not the greatest controller, not the greatest person. I went through the whole business of accepting the fact that I was alcoholic, that my life had become unmanageable. I surrendered to the fact that I couldn't fix myself, and I turned my life over to a power greater than I that could lead me to sanity.

I learned in recovery that we must try to love unselfishly, and not expect anything in return. I was never good at that, but people can change. Susan said that Chuck and I were not natural companions, we would not automatically have sought each other out. But because he's important to Susan, I love him, and now we're good friends.

I know this sounds almost simpleminded, but most truths are simple. When I autograph books for alcoholics who ask me to, I write, "Sobriety is joy."

Nobody gets recovery overnight, and in treatment, we don't

demand that the patient believe, but we ask him to have an open mind. There are so many ways to faith.

Every once in a while, a friend who goes into treatment credits his or her recovery to Leonard and me. We don't accept the credit. Again, we know it's God working through us. One thing is for sure, nobody should go to treatment just to please his wife or his kids or Leonard or me. Unless the alcoholic wants to be sober, he might as well skip it. Leonard and I can sometimes find the words, share the phrases that a patient needs to hear, whether or not he wants to hear them. And God gives us the strength to be willing to face the person's anger when we confront him with truth. That's tough love.

At the beginning of my recovery, I read everything I could find about alcoholism and treatment. I read inspirational material and statistical material. I read pieces that made me think, and I read pieces that made me angry. A friend put me on to a collection called *The Great Texts of the Bible,* and, searching the index for some reference to alcoholism, I found Numbers 32, Verse 23 —"Be sure your sin will find you out"—explicated at great length. The author went on and on about how a drunkard's sin brought its own punishment. "The sin looks out of his bloodshot eyes and grasps his hands until they tremble as with palsy." Well, this treatise was written in the early 1900s, when they didn't know alcoholism was a disease, and not a sin. Today we believe the sin is in not doing something about it.

I have found sobriety brings balance, and balance brings serenity. In recovery, I have sometimes lost this balance, and it usually happens when I am neglecting my spiritual program. Then all the chronic symptoms—envy, resentment, self-pity, anger—of my disease reappear. Like most alcoholics, I handle anger badly, and I try to deal with this by writing out what is making me angry, and when I put it down on paper, I realize how I'm allowing it to disrupt my life. And this realization permits me to move along. I really do believe that God never gives us more than we can handle. But I also believe He expects us to do the footwork, we can't just sit back and wait for Him to dump everything in our laps.

180

All the women who came to Long Beach to help me signed the book they brought me. One of them wrote, "May He hold you in the palm of His hand."

I think He does.

15

My problem is how not to will;
They move most quickly who stand still;
I'm only lost until I see
I'm lost because I want to be.

W. H. Auden

Just to confuse the issue, a postscript to the spirituality discussion. Jim West says no data have ever really been collected to show whether or not people have more difficulty recovering if they can't conceptualize a Higher Power in their lives. He says that, over the years, he's known a great many agnostics, they're making it just fine, and most of them have done it through AA.

Jim West: "I think people are motivated to get better for whatever causes—terrible physical condition, psychosocial condition, occupational condition—there aren't too many of them. And different people interpret Higher Power differently; it doesn't have to be a theological power, it can be the group, it can be a kind of great unknown. The agnostics have to admit there is no proof that there isn't any God, and as far as they are concerned, that's good enough.

"That's why the AA program has endured since 1935, and believe me, it has been battered and pushed and pulled at."

Which reminds me of a joke I sometimes tell in the course of a speech. Mrs. Jones's husband, who was alcoholic, died of the disease. Standing at the graveside, Mrs. Jones received condolences. One casual acquaintance, a Mr. Smith, offered his sympathy and asked the nature of her husband's illness.

Mrs. Jones said Mr. Jones had drunk himself to death.

"Oh," said Mr. Smith, "was he a member of AA?"

"Of course not!" cried Mrs. Jones. "He was never *that* bad!"

Sometimes it's easier to die of drink than to admit to alcoholism and live. If you opt for living, meetings are your lifeline. When I speak at the Center, I tell the patients that. "If you don't do anything else when you leave here, get tied into a good support group. And if you don't like one group, find another or start one with friends who are also recovering. But go, and keep going."

There are self-help groups of all kinds. There are groups for people who can't stop eating, for people who can't stop gambling, for people who are emotionally disturbed, for people who have experienced sexual abuse, for battered wives, for drug addicts and for alcoholics who are *not* affiliated with AA.

The guidelines used by most of these groups are based on the Twelve Steps of AA. And most of these groups practice anonymity. In the case of AA, there were a couple of reasons why this tradition was established. One was to prevent any single individual from purporting to speak for an organization which has never had official spokesmen. People say, "How can it exist?" and the answer is: "Nobody knows." There's a joke about a drunk who was asked, "How does AA work?" "Fine," the drunk said. "Just fine."

Anonymity also protects the reputation of the organization itself. If somebody joins AA, and fails to stay sober, skeptics might say AA is no good. Besides, when the world was younger, and alcoholics were considered the lowest form of animal, nobody mentioned he went to AA because it would have harmed him socially and in the marketplace. It was all right to fall into the gutter, but you didn't dare admit you needed to do something about it.

184

Because it is non-judgmental, because it doesn't ask for a penny from its members and because it works, AA's program has spread all over the world, and we who run treatment centers borrow and steal from its wisdom.

Dolores Hope has been so impressed by the progress of patients at the Center she thinks the program should be given to everyone. "Whether they're alcoholic or not," she says. "There are people suffering, trying to cope with life. And they have to admit there are certain things they are not able to do, certain situations they cannot handle, certain personalities that are diabolical for them to be exposed to. If there was some way that you could treat yourself like an alcoholic, get into this program, that would be wonderful."

Some members of Alcoholics Anonymous do not think treatment centers are necessary for every alcoholic. I've met many alcoholics who have told me they recovered simply by going to AA, without the ministrations of psychiatrists or nutritionists. But because of my own experience at Long Beach, I believe that the concentrated attention you get in a rehab helps do the job faster.

Thirty years ago, there were very few treatment places in the United States; now there are thousands. And they are vitally important because some people who won't go to AA will go to a treatment center where they hope they can be taught how to drink. When they learn this is foolishness, they either leave or hang around and begin to save their lives.

But once they're home again, they need a group. Most of them do, anyway. They need the reinforcement of a group, the sharing of a group, the acceptance of a group helps them to accept themselves as recovering people.

I've told about my first year of meeting with a group of ladies and being afraid to say anything, afraid to sound stupid or foolish. I would walk through the door and my stomach would start to do flip-flops because I was afraid I might be asked to read aloud. Meri Bell did not indulge me in my terrors. "I'll see you in the morning at ten, won't I?" she would say. I was more scared of her than of my stomach, so I would get there by ten. Well, maybe ten-fifteen.

There is almost never a meeting where you don't encounter

miracles. I remember a little girl who was new to the group standing up to tell her story. She said she had been dead drunk six months before, and knew she had to quit, "in order to save my life. And I had to leave the man I loved or the man I thought, in my sickness, I loved. He died of alcoholism two months later. And I didn't take a drink. I've been sober six months, and I'm grateful."

Six months may not sound like much, but it's a good start. There are people who never make six months. They come to meetings faithfully, and then around the fourth or fifth month, they get squirrelly, and go off and drink, and then they come back and try again.

Trying is what it's about. When I got out of Long Beach, I would have been happy to believe the friends who told me I didn't have a drinking problem, it was just the pills that had messed me up. I went to meetings where I was so tense I couldn't hear much that was being said. And then I began to clear and realize that what they were talking about related to me.

Now it's different. I see the other people. We've been through something together. The same way I share a certain understanding with women who have had mastectomies, I share an understanding with recovering alcoholics. I have known what it's like to have my life out of control. There is no support group anywhere in the world where I would feel like a stranger.

That first summer after Long Beach, we were in Vail, and a few women who were recovering alcoholics came up from Denver, and we formed a kind of intimate, friendly group. Some of the women had eight years' sobriety, and to me in my first summer, that was a lifetime. I couldn't imagine anyone who had gone eight years without taking a drink.

The second summer, the group came to Vail again, and we spent a couple of days together, and one of the women, who was working in the field as a counselor at a treatment center, got on the subject of self-honesty. I was still telling myself I had been no more than a social drinker, and all of a sudden, I had an awakening. I knew that my "social" drinking was a fiction, "honest self-deception." I didn't drink to be social, I drank out of a compulsion

I didn't understand. That's alcoholism. And I thought, that's okay, that's what they mean when they say, "More will be revealed to you."

We're still meeting every summer. Each year, the group grows more important to us. We call ourselves the Denver Dolls, and it isn't all talking about recovery either, we spend a lot of time eating, gossiping and shopping.

Eight years ago, there was only one meeting a week in Vail, on Wednesday night. Now there are nineteen in the area. There are meetings at night and at high noon. And when I see that, I'm happy so many more people are finding help.

But the battle is never won. An alcoholic needs an ongoing support system. I remember hearing a woman speak at a conference, and her story was so moving, she was so convincing, so dedicated, and later she drifted away from her support group, drank again and eventually committed suicide.

When you're bereft of your chemicals, you have to learn to cope with that void. You fill it with people, with love, with meetings.

It took me a long time to quit being juvenile, acting immature in my recovery. I kept pulling all these little group-pleasing things to make everybody think I was getting it—oh, yes, look at me, I'm getting it.

Alcoholics are great manipulators, they think they fool people, and I suppose my way of dealing with my inadequacies was to try to look put together and in control. And all the time, I was worrying through everything I had to do, feeling insecure. I was very aware of being just a simple old girl from Grand Rapids, Michigan. I wasn't ashamed of it, but I didn't feel I had the worldly experience and knowledge to be going around meeting queens and maharajahs. I was perfectly well equipped, I'd lived in New York, earned my own way, danced with Martha Graham, but how could I believe it when I did not have—horrors!—a college degree?

Feelings of inadequacy are part of the alcoholic personality. An alcoholic can appear to be very conceited, full of braggadocio,

187

but this is a front. I covered my own feelings of inadequacy by trying to appear very sure of myself.

It worked. Unless you remember that I had to spend my sixtieth birthday in a rehabilitation center.

During those many early meetings, I was advised to be quiet and listen—I didn't really need the advice, you'd have had to horsewhip me to make me take center stage—and I remember certain book study meetings where the paragraph under consideration dealt with self-pity, or anger or resentment. Sometimes the words would hit me right between the eyes. It was like that ad for men's shaving lotion where the guy slaps his face and says, "Thanks, I needed that."

Bring the body and the mind will follow. It can't be repeated often enough. You aren't sure what people are saying, but the information is getting into your computer, and after a while, you have a nice awakening, you begin to understand.

People ask whether or not I had any friends left once I sobered up, whether the people I knew who were still drinking were self-conscious about being around me. Well, my experience is different from the experience of younger people in my support groups. At sixty, most of my friends were not having wild parties.

At home, we still had a bar, we still served drinks, and when I was out with drinkers, it wasn't a problem for me. For some people this can be tough. Most treatment centers advise putting the liquor out of sight and availability until you become more sure of yourself. I remember a big fund-raising event for the Eisenhower Hospital—it was a spring fashion show—and I ordered a tonic and lime, and when I went to drink it, there was vodka in it. I simply asked the waitress to take it away and bring me a plain tonic. I was comfortable with that, because I had gone public. Somebody who hadn't made public the fact that she had stopped drinking might have been intimidated, might have thought, I don't dare send this back because somebody will notice.

If I'm served a dessert like ice cream, and they've poured Kahlúa or crème de menthe over it, and all that liqueur is going to gather in the bottom of the dish, I just leave it and say no, thank you. I don't make a big thing about it.

And I don't turn my glass down. I think it's rude at a nice dinner table set with somebody's good crystal; I just watch for the person who's serving and tell him I don't care for any wine this evening.

You say no, thank you, to spinach if you don't like it, you say no, thank you, to strawberries if they make you break out, what's wrong with saying no, thank you, to a glass of wine?

Anyway, I seem to have kept my old friends, though few of them do any heavy drinking around me. Perhaps it makes *them* uncomfortable. It doesn't make me uncomfortable.

When I first went to meetings, I had been told that these were going to be the people who would mean the most to me, who would always be there for me. I didn't get it. How, all of a sudden, was I going to become a part of this group, when I still had all my old friends and an entirely different life out there?

In time, the question was answered. The men and women in my support groups *have* become very important in my life; they're the ones who understand me when I'm hurting, they're the ones who know what it means to be alcoholic. If I ever felt I was in trouble, they are the people I would go to.

Which doesn't mean I warm to everybody in every group, at every meeting. There are those with whom I will never be friends, and that's all right too. There are people who don't follow the rules, people who gossip. Alcoholics are no different from the general run of human beings. Meri Bell says if you sober up a man who was a horse thief before he started drinking, he may still be a horse thief when he quits drinking.

Meri Bell Sharbutt: "You hear a lot about high-bottom drunks and low-bottom drunks. The only difference between them is economic. The alcoholics you used to hear about were skid row drunks who drank under a bridge, or in a gutter, but there were also little old ladies who passed their days drinking Lydia Pinkham's Extract, which was 60 percent alcohol.

"The bottom is actually soul sickness. When you have gone as far as you can go with your pretense and your façade and you are willing—in Betty's case, with intervention—to get sober. Some people go to AA, some people go to treatment, some people turn to Christian Science, some sign up for aversion therapy, where they give you ipecac, and then make you drink, and you have to watch yourself in a mirror getting sick and throwing up. I think people get sober anywhere, anytime.

"But alcohol is cunning, it will wait for you forever. If I took a drink today, I would be thirty years along in the progression of my disease. So I go to meetings because that's the way I remind myself that by myself I could not stay sober. Many people have tried. They've done my research for me."

Meri Bell was forty-three when she got sober, and I was sixty. Now we have people sixteen coming to our meetings, because the loose structure of our society allows a sixteen-year-old to destroy himself in a very short time.

We see so many new people coming into groups now, and there isn't always enough time given to the beginners, to tell them the things that will help them, to make them understand that sometimes they have to stand still when they don't want to. They're used to going full tilt, and when they learn that's not the way you get sober, it's at great emotional cost.

It takes so long to learn that you can't have it all at once.

I have a friend—he's *not* a youngster—who confided in me one evening at a dinner party. He told me how he had stopped drinking. He said he couldn't bear to continue to wake up in the morning embarrassed by what he remembered he had done the night before. And it was just as bad when he couldn't remember at all, when he had a total blackout.

He'd heard about AA, and the book they considered their bible. He bought a copy, read it and worked a program on his own.

He was a very disciplined man, and he was able to do this, but he might have found an even richer experience if he had joined with other recovering people.

We can understand our disease and accept it more easily when we are with people who understand *us*.

I remember the first time I was asked to lead a meeting. I thought I was expected to tell my story and I sat up until two o'clock in the morning writing about what it was like then, what had happened, what it is like now. The next morning when I got up to be Madam Chairperson, I read through the agenda, and I saw the part where I was to start the meeting, but nowhere did it say a word about my telling my story.

I told it anyway. I said, "I stayed up until two o'clock in the morning writing this. If you don't want to hear it, leave and come back later."

I have learned from all kinds of groups, from meetings with conservative middle-aged women and meetings with drug-using kids who have come right off the street. That's sort of like walking into a jungle, when you're not used to it. The four-letter words are just like you hear in the movies. What they're saying is okay, but the way they say it puts me off. It takes me about fifteen minutes to settle in. At one meeting, a girl who noticed Meri Bell looking disapproving came up to her later and said, "You don't like the way I talk, do you?" Meri Bell said no, she didn't. "If you're going to clean up your life," she said, "I think you should clean up your mouth."

On the other hand, the conservative-appearing ladies used to amaze me too. You'd see these women who looked like they had never done anything risque or out of the mainstream, and they'd start talking about their drinking, and how they used to be pretty wild in their heyday. One of them whom I admired from afar—she made profound, all-encompassing statements about recovery and staying sober and getting your life in shape—always intimidated me. I thought she was so stern. And then I heard her telling a woman who had slipped not to worry, she was doing great, and I thought, how loving she is, and how easy it is to read somebody wrong.

You can find a meeting no matter where you are in the United States. You can find a meeting anywhere in the world. Some of the people who come to the Betty Ford Center for

191

treatment go back to Australia, Italy, France, and they join—or start—support groups of recovering alcoholics.

On the anniversary of the day I had been sober seven years, I went off to my women's group, and afterward there was the usual monthly luncheon. As the day approached I hadn't been very impressed with the idea of seven years—so it's another year—but when I got up to speak, to thank these comrades, these other recovering women, I was just overcome with love and gratitude. I could hardly talk, the tears were welling up in my eyes, my throat was tight, and I thought, God speaks to us in such strange ways.

The learning in meetings never stops. I've heard Muriel, with twenty-seven years of sobriety, and Meri Bell, with thirty, say, "I just can't believe that more is still being revealed to me."

It comes over you like a wave. Suddenly you know something you could not have accepted knowing a year, a month, even a day before.

My early drinking became clear to me in such a wave. I had done most of it when I was alone at night. Why hadn't I read good books? Why hadn't I developed my mind? Why, at the end of the day, did I watch television, and drink?

Because I was physically exhausted, that was why, because I'd been charging around after four kids all day, because I wanted to be lazy. The idea that I might *need* to be lazy had never occurred to me, I didn't like to think of it; I am so much an A personality, so energetic, so determined to get things done and keep going. But in one of those times of revelation, I was finally able to forgive myself for watching Lucille Ball when I could have been reading Spinoza. The hell with Spinoza, say I.

I read an interview with Richard Pryor in which he told how meetings had changed him. He said that even after his accident, free-basing cocaine, despite the fact that he'd been scared he was going to die, he had not stayed clean or sober. And then he went to visit a friend. "He was in the hospital for drugs. They had these group meetings. I was sitting there listening to all the people talk and I *heard* something. And I said, 'S—t. This is good here. Remind you of anybody, Rich?' And the more I went to visit, the more I was like a clandestine participant in the recovery of a drug addict. And one day I stood up and said I was a drug addict."

There it is. You hear it when you're ready, when you're able. For people who aren't sure, but who are making the first tentative steps toward deciding whether or not they're alcoholic, or addicted to some other drug, the Alcohol Awareness Hours that are held over at the Annenberg Center can be instructive, not to say lifesaving.

I first learned about the Alcohol Awareness Hours when I came back from Long Beach. They were held on Saturday mornings by Joe Cruse and Del and Meri Bell Sharbutt. They had been doing this for several years, in order to teach the community at large about alcoholism—what it was, and that recovery was possible.

Meri Bell Sharbutt: "The first three years of its existence, Joe, Del and I footed the bill for the Alcohol Awareness Hour. We called speakers—recovering alcoholics who were well known—and said, 'Here is what we're trying to do. Will you help us?' They came. We had no money, so they came at their own expense. We had them stay at our homes, we arranged golf games for them, we took them to dinner.

"That was about ten years ago. Our Alcohol Awareness Hour was the first, and now there are many, all over the country. Ours is a community effort. It is free for everyone. I don't care if you are social dynamite or at the bottom of the heap, you are welcome. We are education and information. We are trying to remove the stigma from the word 'alcoholic,' and the fact that we're still in existence means we're doing something right.

"We get the major part of our funding now from the Eisenhower Auxiliary and we reach people who would be frightened or embarrassed to go to an AA meeting. They come, and often, they come back."

A friend of mine remembers the first time he went to an awareness hour. He was wearing sunglasses. "I think everybody walks into the first meetings with sunglasses," he says. "You think,

193

'They'll never know me,' even though you might look like a truck. A truck with sunglasses."

"I went, and I was looking at the directory downstairs, and a little old lady, one of the hospital volunteers, came over and said, 'Can I help you, son?' And I said, 'Yeah, I was trying to see where they're gonna have the Alcohol Awareness Hour.' 'Oh,' she says, in a voice I was convinced at the time carried clear to downtown Rancho Mirage. 'You mean where all those alkies meet?'

"I cringed. It was just like somebody threw a bucket of water on me. 'They meet on the second floor,' she said, 'take that elevator.'

"So I said thanks, and I skulked down to the elevator, got on, and a couple of people came aboard wearing these big round buttons that say, 'Some of My Best Friends Are Alcoholics.' I stood in the back of the elevator, I didn't want to associate with them.

"But anyway, I went to some of those meetings, and they were very good. A marvelous informational thing. They always ask people to put up their hands if this is the first time they've been there, and always about half the room puts up hands.

"Out of those meetings comes a lot of awareness—literally. That was a fantastic thing that Joe and Del and Meri Bell started. They have athletes, actors, doctors, excellent speakers. And anybody can go. From anywhere. It's marvelous."

Every time there's a new book on alcoholism, Del and Meri Bell snare the author as a speaker. Many of the doctors they bring in to lecture are themselves recovering alcoholics, and the Auxiliary of Eisenhower serves coffee and doughnuts; showing up for the Awareness Hour has become a popular thing to do on a Saturday morning.

In no way does it intimidate. It's just "Listen to what so-and-so has to say, it will help to educate you about the disease."

Del Sharbutt always greets the audience, and says something like "Please don't call us reformed alcoholics, you wouldn't talk about a 'reformed' cancer patient, or a 'reformed' heart patient." Or he may explain that, according to the U.S. Department of

194

Agriculture, Americans drink more alcohol than milk. And another Alcohol Awareness Hour is off and running.

Once, speaking at an Awareness Hour, Leonard summed up the dynamics of the thing in a brilliant way.

Leonard Firestone: "Last winter, I was asked to speak at a dinner at the Monterey Country Club, and my subject was to be the Bob Hope Cultural Center. They told me about ten days before the dinner that they had a hundred reservations. Right after that, somebody put up a golf cart as a door prize, and they got another hundred reservations.

"On the night of the dinner, I said to the crowd, 'I don't know how many of you came to hear me, and how many of you came to win the golf cart.' But it really didn't make any difference, because they were there, and they got the message. And in some ways, I think the Awareness Hour operates a little on that kind of basis.

"We don't know exactly why people come. Some may be alcoholics, and want to see if they can get help; others may think they might be alcoholics, and come to see if they can learn something. Or they come because a friend is in trouble, and they'll learn something that can help the friend. In any event, they come. And they get the message."

That's what all of us, in our separate ways, try to do. Pass along the message. And it is through this sharing, through our own joy in recovery, that we attract others to the program we embrace.

It doesn't matter whether you start interacting with a group at a treatment center or in AA or during an Alcohol Awareness Hour; it doesn't matter whether you come through the front door or the side door or the back door; it doesn't matter whether you meet in a church basement or in a community center—there is help out there for anyone who wants it.

16

The wine of Love is music,
  And the feast of Love is song:
And when Love sits down to the banquet,
  Love sits long:

Sits long and arises drunken,
  But not with the feast and the wine;
He reeleth with his own heart,
  That great, rich Vine.

                James Thomson

I'm here to say that *you* can reel with your own heart and your own brain too once you quit believing that only alcohol or drugs can make you joyful.

Sometimes, I'm almost sorry for people who *haven't* been alcoholic, because I know things that a person who's never been sick doesn't know. I had to climb over hurdles. I had to experience the disease, be sick with it and then experience recovery.

I've said this before, but it's worth repeating: When you recover, you are weller than well. Your life takes on a different quality. You are able to accomplish more than you ever dreamed you could. In the eight years since my recovery, I have not needed to use drugs or alcohol to help me live my life, I have been free to make choices, and there has been such an exhilaration in that, such an inner feeling of self-fulfillment and self-

197

worth. I can't imagine anything more valuable, more satisfying. In recovery, you have a completely new lease on life, and that's what a person who's never been sick has not experienced.

Sometimes, in your wellness, it's hard to credit how sick you used to be. When Joe Cruse finally brought back the mountain of pills he had taken away from me before Long Beach, I put them in a closet off my bedroom lest I forget. After a while, I could smell that odor of old drugs. It was noxious, so I moved them to another closet in a spare room. And the aroma still grew. Finally, I put the whole mess in a huge plastic bag and stored it outside in an old storage cupboard, so I would always remember how sick I had been. It's strange, the odds and ends of your life that wind up in those cupboards.

I'm grateful that's all behind me. Sheika remembers when I returned to Vail that summer after treatment.

Sheika Gramshammer: "It was like you opened the door, and the sunshine came in, and the warmth with the sunshine. And the thing which was sheltered and covered up for so long, her identity, came through.

"There were times when we had said, 'Betty, why don't you lie down?' or 'Why don't you get help?' But this is something she had to do herself, she had to be ready for it, and I think the time when she did it, it was her time to come out."

Since I've "come out," I've talked so much there may be people who wish I'd go back in, but I need to share the sunshine and warmth that came through when the door opened.

Leonard feels the same way. We both know there are other treatment centers that accomplish as much good as the BFC, but you don't hear about them as frequently, so we talk them up too. One of them—Turnoff, which I mentioned in earlier chapters—is run by a man named Sam Hardy and his wife, Ann.

Leonard Firestone: "There are, I think, different kinds of rehabs. Now Sam Hardy takes kids under eighteen. A lot of times, they're referred by the courts. Sam is a green-thumb kind of guy, he just knows kids, and he gets them straightened out. He sent one boy down to a lady who needed housework done and was going to pay by the hour. The boy came back, the lady called Sam the next day and said, 'I think this boy you sent down stole my clock.' Sam said, 'Okay, I'll find out.' He asked the kid, and the kid said yes, he'd done it. Sam said, 'Well, let me tell you what you do. You take that clock back to that lady and you tell her you're returning her clock, you did steal it, you're sorry, and you want to make amends. And then you do whatever she asks you to do. And when you've done that, forget it. It's finished.'

"A judge wouldn't do that, I wouldn't think of that, but that's what Sam told the kid. The kid had been terrified he'd have to go back to Juvenile Hall, but Sam let him handle it, and he came back and got straightened out.

"Turnoff is filled with every leftover sofa and chair that anybody would contribute, but it's cozy, it's clean, the kids are great-looking, and they have dignity. It's exciting to see that kind of operation. It's in an old house, but anybody could be happy staying there."

Lost Heads is another wonderful rehab. It's in the high desert, and when Rick Mesa took over the management, it was a mess. Nobody had kept books, there wasn't any money, Rick didn't know how he was going to be able to feed the patients. He said they had four cars, three of them didn't run, the buildings were leaking, there weren't enough beds, and he was looking to see how they could get some people who had public visibility interested, and also get some financial support.

My first thought was the people I had worked with in getting the Betty Ford Center started. I made appointments. I went to Leonard and Ed Johnsen and said, "This guy needs help. What do you suppose we can do for him?"

It was right up their alley. Both of them wanted to work on a place that might provide treatment for the less privileged, for those who could afford to pay little or nothing. They came out, took a look and began to figure out what had to be done.

199

Ed Johnsen: "There was nothing there but a couple of old shacks; one was the size of a three-car garage and six ladies were living in it with one bathroom and one little gas heater. The cold hung on there, the ceiling was falling, and there was no privacy. It's pretty tough to get dignity out of a situation like that. You're already feeling pretty down on yourself for having got into that situation.

"We put up two new buildings in one weekend. We began work at dawn on December 7, 1985. We had a lot of help. A fellow donated two fireplaces, a lady I know who has a carpet mill in Idaho gave us five hundred yards of carpet, a lumberman donated $15,000 worth of wood, and dozens of people contributed their labor.

"It was like a barn raising, neighbors getting together and saying, let's go over and help old George. And it was a thrill. I remember seeing one man who had just checked in the night before, and he was in bad shape. He was a former builder, a carpenter, but on Saturday all he did was watch. He was detoxing right then. By Sunday afternoon he was bending over, picking up some scrap and taking it out of the way. Two weeks later, I went over, and he had his leather belt on, he was stripped down to his shorts, and he had organized a team to build auxiliary wardrobes to go alongside the lockers.

"On the morning of December 7, some ladies volunteered to come over and cook breakfast, and we had about eighty people show up to work. We worked all day Saturday and all day Sunday, and by Sunday night we had both buildings erected, each big enough to hold twenty beds. What would have cost over $300,000 as a commercial project ended up costing only about $75,000, due to the wonderful spirit of the community.

"We did pay some people. You can get carried away with the romance of volunteer help, and we knew we had to have enough people there to make sure the things went up properly. They're really very nice-looking, well-constructed buildings. They'll be there forever. The patients are walking on five feet of air. I'm pleased. I think we'll have a dedication after a while."

It was such a good endeavor. One couple gave Rick cash for a van, and Jerry and I sent money at Christmas. I wrote to people I'd normally have sent Christmas flowers and said we were making a donation to Lost Heads Ranch in their names. Then Lost Heads wrote to thank everybody, so now the Lost Heads mailing list is a good bit longer. I thought that was better than my sending flowers to a lot of people who didn't need flowers. It was a little manipulative, but it was for a good cause.

In addition to manipulation, one of my character defects is that I'm always trying to be what I think people want me to be. Which is available. I've had to learn there are going to be more people asking for my time than I can possibly see or please. I have to get used to that. I'm not the only one there for those people, there are plenty of others who know more and can counsel better, and I have to accept that, and so do they.

Still, I think wanting to respond to other people is a strength. If someone comes over to talk to me, I don't believe in cutting that person off short. I try to listen. I've learned a lot that way.

Despite ourselves, we learn. I've learned to recognize when I'm not working my program. Anger interferes, and so does overload. Sometimes I get short with those closest to me, like Ann Cullen, who has worked with me for almost six years and whom I love as I love my own daughter. Yet I know I have hurt her at times by being impatient, by expecting too much, or because I was having resentment about something else and I had to take it out on somebody. Somebody I knew I could take advantage of. And then I regret it. Because whatever it was wasn't important enough to get that upset about.

Mostly, these things happen when I'm too busy, when I'm trying to do too much in too short a time.

I don't think I'm as crazy as I was in the first years of my sobriety. I remember the weekend Leonard went off to treatment, and he and Nicky had been expecting houseguests—Pat and Al Haig—and Nicky said to me, "Will you please take over the entertaining?"

When I went to bed Friday night, I had a hundred things

falling all over each other in my head. The next day, I wanted to get up and go over to the Awareness Hour, because Muriel Zink was speaking. And then I would have to rush home and be hostess at a luncheon for the Haigs, and I was concerned with the flowers, the menu, the china, the place mats, everything.

In addition, Saturday night, we were going to a black-tie dinner, to which the Haigs were also invited. It was in honor of some of Queen Elizabeth's entourage, one of them a lady-in-waiting who had accompanied the Queen when she visited us in Washington in 1976.

I couldn't sleep. I was worrying about what to wear the following night. At three o'clock in the morning, I got up and went into my closet and looked at my evening dresses. I didn't want to be caught in something I'd worn at the White House during the Queen's visit. It was silly, but typical of me at that stage of my recovery. These people were special guests of the Annenbergs, and I didn't want to show up in the same dress I'd worn three years before.

At three-thirty in the morning, I was still trying on clothes. I don't do that anymore.

There are other things I don't do either. If I have a problem with household help, I don't upset my husband by complaining to him over the phone when he's thousands of miles away. I assume responsibility, because I'm supposed to be able to run my house.

A while back, one of the people who worked for us quit when we had houseguests coming the next day, and I said to myself, let it go, you can't do anything about it. At an earlier stage of my sobriety, I would have been so consumed with anger it could have made me physically ill.

Even though Jerry is my main support system, these days I try not to burden him. He was gone when our dog Liberty died, and I told him because he was anxious about her and was asking. But I try to avoid running to him with trivia, the way I once might have.

Susan always said I was good in a crisis; it was the little everyday things I couldn't handle. When Jerry was defeated for the presidency in the election of 1976, I had to fill in and make the concession speech and the remarks on television and so forth. The kids were very upset, and Jerry had lost his voice in the final days of the campaign, so it was up to me. Now I'm trying to learn to handle the little everyday things as well.

When I told Susan that Liberty had died, she cried, and then Tyne cried, but I didn't. Lib was a very dear old dog, and I was glad she wasn't suffering anymore.

I've had to learn to let go of creatures I've loved, people I've loved. I guess even my attitudes toward death have changed with sobriety.

I had no serenity when my mother died as the result of a cerebral hemorrhage. I was angry. I cried myself to sleep nights because I hadn't been able to reach her before she died. My plane was delayed because of mechanical problems, and I damned the circumstances. I knew my mother would never have been happy living as an invalid, but her death came soon after I married Jerry, and I had a lot of guilt about that. Maybe I had required too much of her, put too much stress on her at the time.

I don't really believe that myself; she was crazy about Jerry, and she did everything she could to make the wedding the way Jerry and I wanted it. But afterward, I worried that I had been more demanding of my mother than I was of Jerry, that I expected more of her.

When my children were born, they had no maternal grandparents, and that bothered me, because my grandparents had died before I was born. It took me a long time to let go of all that anger and guilt and resentment.

But because grandparents have always seemed special to me, I'm now living out the role of grandmother with delight. I love my five little granddaughters, I hope someday to love my grandsons. I don't want to spoil and ruin them, but I want to get right to the verge of it.

The last Ford baby, Hannah Gayle, was born in September 1985. We were up in Colorado, and all day I kept calling Gayle's mother. (Gayle was to have a caesarian section, so the date was set.)

"Have you heard anything from the hospital or Mike?" I would say, and Gayle's mother would say, "Not a word. I just can't imagine what's going on, but maybe the doctor had some emergency he had to take care of first."

I finally went out and had my hair done, and while I was gone, Mike called the office and spoke to Jerry's assistant. "Do you think they'll accept another girl?" he said, kidding.

We accepted her. Gladly.

In 1985, the whole family came up to the house in Beaver Creek for Christmas week. We built the place in the mountains, a few miles from Vail; it started out to be small, but we kept adding on—a recreation room, an office, a playroom, bedroom and bath in the loft for the grandchildren—until we achieved absolute magnificence.

It was the best Christmas we ever had, and I keep contrasting it with the Christmas seven years earlier when the children were pussyfooting around and whispering to each other in corners about what they were going to do with me, their alcoholic parent.

In 1985, everybody got along. There was no undercurrent of conflicting personalities. And that's surprising when you think there were fourteen people living together. Steve had brought a friend, there was a brand-new three-month-old baby, and not everybody was thinking about eating at the same time, or going to church at the same time, yet it all worked.

The kids played games and enjoyed having dinner together, and I was entirely relaxed in spite of the fact that they were drinking our very best wine, at forty-five dollars a bottle, and leaving the cheap stuff. The argument was: "Well, we wanted to leave a lot of one kind for you, Mother, so you'd be sure to have enough for a big dinner party. We're drinking up the rare bottles because there are only two or three of them."

I was able to laugh and be comfortable with their drinking, I didn't feel I needed to be in control of the situation, I could let them have their good time and contentedly go off to bed with my husband.

I was well enough to let my children run their own lives.

There were so many special things about that week. On Christmas Eve, while I was out doing some last-minute shopping, it began to snow. It always takes a few flakes on my eyelashes to make me feel really Christmasy. Later, at home, the little girls, Tyne, Heather, Rebekah and Sarah—everybody but Hannah—came downstairs in their pajamas and robes and hung up their stockings. And we put out carrots and lettuce for the reindeer to eat, and cookies and milk for Santa Claus and his helpers. Early Christmas morning the girls found an empty glass and plate with a note from Santa that said Uncle Jack and Uncle Steve were bad boys and weren't going to get anything. They loved that, even though they worship Uncle Jack and Uncle Steve. They call Jack the Tickle Monster.

We went caroling too. We rode in a hay-filled wagon over to the Children's Fountain in Vail. We were bundled up in big fur blankets, and we sang all the way. At the beginning of the Christmas program at the fountain, one of the grandchildren pushed the switch to light the tree. We've been lighting trees in Vail ever since Jerry was Vice President.

Santa Claus was waiting at the tree, and at first, our girls wouldn't have anything to do with him. One of them grabbed my arm and said, "He's not going to ho-ho-ho, is he? I don't like it when he ho-ho-ho's."

By the time we got back in the wagon, Santa was their best friend. It was a question of who was going to sit next to him, and they never let him have a minute to himself or let any other—non-Ford—kids get closer than necessary.

Before we left for Vail, there had been more serenading from small girls back in Palm Springs. John Schwarzlose took his daughter Rachel and her Brownie troop (there must have been a dozen six-year-olds) to the Center to sing carols for the patients. I'd invited them to stop by our house afterward and perform for us. So they came, and stood on the front steps and launched into "Rudolph, the Red-Nosed Reindeer." I came out to listen, and after the song, I congratulated them, and Lisa Schwarzlose,

John's wife, asked each little girl to introduce herself. Then she gestured toward me. "Now do all you girls know who this is?"

"Mrs. Ford," one of them said.

"But do you know who Mrs. Ford is?"

"She's the lady who's named after the Betty Ford Center," said the little girl.

Sometimes I feel that's true. The Center runs me, rules my life. But I like it that way. Though sometimes I stand back and look at myself sitting in some tycoon's office, trying to interest him in an assistance program to help his alcoholic employees, and I think, why couldn't I have taken up golf? Then at least I'd be outside on this pretty afternoon.

Almost everyone has some alcoholism in the family. But lots of executives don't believe they could possibly have it within their business organizations. I had a conversation with a clothing magnate—he has thousands of employees—and he said, "Oh, we just don't have alcoholics in our business." And I thought, this man doesn't drink, so he doesn't see any drinkers. After we got through talking, he said, "Well, you know, I have been sort of blind. I'm going to take another look." There are some companies that don't want to be aware of the problem, because they don't want to deal with it. Their policy is to fire the alcoholic rather than offer rehabilitation, even though it is financially more sound to rehabilitate a trained worker than to let him or her go.

But I keep badgering them and hoping. I've turned into a splendid haranguer of all kinds of audiences, even though I'm still terrified when I speak. Always, I anticipate the possibility of falling on my face. Always, I know there comes that time when you don't do well. And I want to do well. I think whether or not a speech comes across has to do with my preparation, and my conviction that what I'm telling the audience is something they need—and want—to hear.

Jerry was a big factor in convincing me that I knew more about my subject than my listeners, so why should I be scared? (Somebody once asked Ethel Merman if she was scared when she went on stage. She looked dumbfounded. "Why should *I* be scared?" she said. "If they could do it, *they'd* be up here.")

At this point, I've had to educate myself in order to educate others. I've spoken to people in the insurance field, to doctors, to religious groups. I started a whole new career when I was sixty years old, a career of recovery.

The nice thing is that now I know I can make a mistake or two before I'm through with this world, and it won't mean I'm unfit to live. I'm just not as frightened as I used to be.

Ann Cullen: "When I first started working for Mrs. Ford, she was about to hit the trail to raise money for the Betty Ford Center, which gave her the impetus to get out there and start doing a lot of public speaking. But she was scared to death. If she had to talk for more than five minutes, she would not sleep for the three nights before the event, and she would be sick to her stomach. She would just be a wreck. Now, she talks for forty-five minutes, and it's 'No, no, they can't take me off yet, I still have things to tell these people.'

"She's much more comfortable now standing up in front of a group, she is more sure that people will listen to what she has to say."

There is something about the challenge of public speaking that's similar to the challenge I once felt about whether I should or shouldn't take a drink or a pill. For me, it was a little like living on the edge, and I liked that in my life.

Today, I get that same kind of exhilaration from standing up and trying to give a good talk, or interview, from trying to erase the stigma associated with the words "alcoholic" and "addict." If I could help remove even one dot above one *i* in those words, I would feel I had proved myself.

Ann Cullen: "I think a lot of the old anxiety was camouflage. She thought if everybody saw the perfect outside, they wouldn't ask questions about what was going on inside. There were a couple of times when hair was the ultimate thing that happened around here, and Mrs. Ford almost lost some of it, because I was going to snatch her bald.

"Seven years ago, she had two hair appointments every week, every Tuesday afternoon, every Friday afternoon. She would not go out the front door if there was a hair out of place, or something the matter with the way she was dressed, or her purse did not match her shoes or whatever. Now she can do with one hair appointment a week, and if she misses that, it's no big deal. Last year, when she went to the Bob Hope Classic Ball (she had been busy getting ready to have her foot operated on), she actually wore a dress that was wrinkled. To a big social event! That was a major breakthrough."

I always thought if I looked good to other people, then I must be okay, and that got me off the hook of having to realize that maybe I wasn't okay. Working through support groups of recovering people, I have learned the value of *being* okay, rather than just *looking* okay.

It's funny, back when I had a little sobriety, I had a discussion with one of my oldest friends in Washington and she said my hair always looked exasperatingly perfect on television. "Why don't you come on with it messed up once in a while?" And I thought, defensively, well, I wouldn't go on television with my hair looking like yours usually does.

But I like my hair less structured now, a little easier, which I suppose is also symbolic of letting go. I did attend the last Bob Hope Ball in a wrinkled dress. It was a gold lamé affair and it had a voluminous skirt that takes forever to press. Ann offered to do it, but I said, "No, they'll just think it's pleated," and she couldn't believe her ears. She said a couple of years ago, I'd have been hysterical if my dress had been in that condition, and I'm sure she's right.

My priorities have changed, and I guess your personality changes with your priorities. I wasn't going to make any grand entrance at the Bob Hope Ball, it wasn't a Betty Ford party, Jerry and I were going to be there as support for Bob and Dolores, because they were our friends.

The changes that come with recovery come in every area of

your life. I no longer care so much about people pleasing, I tell the truth to—and about—doctors, I've stopped denying I'm an alcoholic, I even travel lighter. Jerry used to say, *"I* don't have to take ten bags to spend two hours like some people I know." Even in my early sobriety, I needed a backup dress for a speech, because what if the zipper broke, or I caught my heel in my hem. Now I just pick a dress and go. It's a small thing, but a sign that I'm more self-assured. Even my brother Bill, who always thought I was nice, thinks I'm nicer now.

Bill Bloomer: "She has a great thoughtfulness and consideration of people, and she's always had that to some extent, but now more than ever. And her life has got meaning and direction and stability beyond my greatest imagination. You know, there are a lot of alcoholics in this world, 10 percent of the people in our country are chemical dependents, and so few of them turn their disease to some good. Or as much good as she has.

"Jerry is so proud of what she's doing; he sat in this room in Scottsdale and all he talked about was what Betty was accomplishing. When I tell people I'm Betty Ford's brother, they say, 'I just love your sister and what she's done,' and it makes me feel good."

If only everyone could speak so wisely!

But seriously, I think these last few years have been my best years, and that in itself is success. Everything keeps getting better.

Scenes with the grandchildren play in my mind. Hannah's christening. A birthday party Tyne and Heather gave for Jack, during which Tyne pushed Jerry, fully dressed, into the pool. When he surfaced, glasses, watch, wallet dripping, he swam silently to one side, walked up the steps, water sloshing out of his shoes. "That wasn't very nice, Tyne," he said. I was tickled. It was his dear, darling Tyne who had done it, and he never can get very mad at her, or any of his granddaughters, but Jack swears the temperature in the pool rose ten degrees.

You can sit outside our dining room and look across the pool and the fountain at two layers of mountains, dark ones in front, light ones behind. There are olive trees and palms and oranges and lemons and grapefruits and roses growing under a bright blue sky. It smells sweet.

And there are other sweetnesses in my life. A while ago, I got a letter from my friend Betz Hutchison. She enclosed a check to the Center. She wrote, "The folk art business did very well this last year. I had been putting a bit aside for a nice piece of Georgian copper. Then I did some long and hard thinking. An old piece of copper is just a thing. It is people, not things, that are life's most valued treasures. Betty, I hope this will help someone, even in a very small way, to regain control of his or her life."

Something like that makes me want to work harder.

There have been blows as well as joys. Last year, Pam Wilder, one of the women who brought the group to me at Long Beach, died of cancer, and so did my darling Nicky Firestone. I think about Nicky every day, not because she was perfect, but because we were neighbors, and relied on each other, and loved each other.

Just before Christmas, Nicky became critically ill. The doctor told me no one but family could see her, and there was nothing I could do. Jerry advised me to go on to Beaver Creek, where our children and grandchildren were coming for the holidays, and where he would join me later.

I flew to Denver. It was one of those days when the air shimmers. The sun was shining, and at one point, the clouds separated and it was almost like a pathway to heaven. I sat there in my quietness, in my love of Nicky, and I felt she had been released.

I had to let go, and let God.

A long time after I had been in treatment at Long Beach, Joe Pursch had a patient come to him at Care Manor. He was a big burly beer distributor, and he said, "I'm here because of Betty Ford. My wife said, 'Look, if even a woman can do it, you ought to be able to do it.'"

Even a woman can do it. A man can do it. A teenager can do

it, and so can an octogenarian. At our Third Alumni Reunion last November, more than eight hundred former BFC patients who had done it came together, and that was a weekend I will never forget.

17

Because the birthday of my life is come . . .
Christina Rossetti

We took 840 reservations for the Saturday-night dinner—840! It was unbelievable to me that we could have that kind of turnout for an anniversary. They came from the desert close by and from faraway places. We filled the Grand Ballroom of Marriott's Rancho Las Palmas. To me it was absolutely astounding. I saw BFC alumni from Hawaii, from New York, from Florida, from Canada, and the celebration of everyone's sobriety made us all buoyant, we bounced along the whole weekend on a giant high.

Saturday morning, the Awareness Hour was held in the Annenberg Center Auditorium, which seats maybe 450. It was full.

Right at the beginning, I thanked the alumni for coming, and said how good it made me feel to look out and see all of them, and then Leonard spoke, and Del Sharbutt spoke, and so did the president of our alumni association, who had been sober for two years. He said he had come to the Betty Ford Center "basically to learn how to drink and work on my tan. And I was only able to accomplish one of those two objectives."

After the formal program, volunteers stood up and told how their lives had changed, they just stood and talked, without mikes, from wherever they were in the auditorium, and it was wonderful.

One after another, they shared their stories.

A man said he'd first come to the Center out of fear, but that in the midst of all his fear, there had been a seed of hope, small as a mustard seed, and that hope had grown, and he had found recovery.

A woman said she'd been wrestling with a drinking problem all her life, "and was scared to death somebody was going to find out I was an alcoholic." Then she'd read about my going into treatment, and said, "One of these days I'm gonna have to do that myself."

She remembered making New Year's resolutions every January 1. "I would say, 'I hope I'll find some happiness this year,' but I never had much happiness. Now I do. I have been sober for nine months, and it's wonderful. I have been frightened, scared, afraid, the whole nine yards, but I have finally found some peace of mind."

There was a girl who'd had a drinking and a drug problem, and had never thought "that I was good enough, or that I helped enough, or that I got enough." She had found out through treatment that "it's okay to feel good, it's okay to smile, it's okay to love and be loved."

There was a young man who said he'd been so desperate to come into treatment that when he'd been told the fee was "fifty-five," he'd said, "Fine, fifty-five thousand dollars is no problem, I'll pay anything." Advised that the fee was fifty-five *hundred* dollars, he'd been shocked. "I thought it was a mistake, because of the movie stars who had come here. I thought this was *the* place, and you had to pay a lot of money."

When he went home after treatment, he was still in trouble. "I thought I had a very secure job. I was president of a company that my father owned. But within fifteen minutes of my being back in the office, he said, 'I don't want you around here anymore, you're fired.' Two days later, the girl I was living with left. She took off with another guy."

This young man said he had started going to support group meetings—"I averaged a hundred eighty meetings in ninety days"—and through them, he had begun to experience "a clarity.

And the talent I didn't think I had came back." He said he'd been able, in recovery, to change the "negativity I've had all my life" into something positive. "Now, when I put out positive, I get positive back."

Every story revealed a marvel.

There was a very pregnant girl who had been in treatment with her husband. You could see their joy, and without recovery, it's a joy they might have missed. The husband said he'd used alcohol and drugs from an early age. "They seemed to diminish those pains I was feeling inside. And everyone would say, 'Look at him, he's so together,' and on the inside, I'm going, 'Hey, man, I'm dying, there's something killing me.'

"But this recovery is contagious. I had a friend who came into the program several months before I did, and when I got to the point where I just didn't want to live anymore, something brought me to his office, and we sat and talked, and three hours later, I was here at the Betty Ford Center seeing if I was sick enough for them to help me.

"They told me I was okay, and they loved me. When I went home, weeks later, I had an idea I'd have a sweet, warm, wonderful relationship with my wife, but it didn't quite work like that. I had to recover from my disease of alcoholism and drug dependence, and then I had to recover from the disease of emotional dependence on that other person. As time goes by, I've come to realize I can be in love with someone without being emotionally dependent on her, and that's just part of the freedom and joy that this program has brought me. If I hadn't come to the Center I'd probably be dead, but today I'm alive and real glad to be here."

The weekend was filled with events. There were brushup workshops at the Center, and we had the groundbreaking for the new, twenty-bed wing to be called Fisher Hall, and everywhere, you could see former patients milling about, embracing with bear hugs, greeting one another.

On Saturday night, the ballroom looked beautiful for the dinner. My friend Mary Fisher—she and her family contributed toward Fisher Hall—had done a terrific job with the decorations. Each table had a BFC medallion set in the center on a round, flat mirror, and the lights of the room bounced off the mirrored centerpieces and flared upward, so that every few feet, on the ceiling, there appeared a big, diffused image of a medallion. Those reflections must have come from the angle of the lights, but there was something almost mystical about it.

And there were balloons, and people dressed in their best, and again we heard brief talks—inspiring, touching, funny—from those who had been asked to tell how their lives in sobriety were going. One drug addict said he'd learned humility while working in a cemetery. "There's forty thousand bodies in that thing," he said, "and a lot of the young people were there because of alcohol and drugs, and that scared me. It made me realize how serious this disease is. And when I was at the Betty Ford Center, I really learned the tools to recovery."

People thanked the counselors who had seen them through their ordeals, they thanked their families, they thanked us listeners for letting them share. "I'm grateful to all the people associated with the Betty Ford Center," said one woman. "For the love and acceptance I felt from the first day. And I'm grateful to God for staying with me when I was lost, and leading me from the depths of hopelessness to the joy I have in recovery."

A former cocaine addict said he had believed he could wing his way through the Center and get back to his drugs. He was shocked when a counselor searched his suitcase and took away his Old Spice. "I said, 'What's the matter? You don't want me to smell good in here?' He said, 'There's alcohol in this Old Spice.' I said, 'I'm a drug addict, I don't drink, especially not Old Spice.' He took it anyway.

"Then I went to see the nurse, who dug out my last gram of cocaine from where I'd hidden it. Thank God."

Instead of getting back to his drugs, he'd gone on to save his life, his marriage, his career. "It's wonderful to be home," he said. "And the Betty Ford Center for me is home."

For me, that night, the Grand Ballroom of the Marriott was home. I was moved to see people, some of whom I remembered as gray-faced, blotchy, burnt-out, now thriving, pink-cheeked, clear-eyed, happy.

But a great poet once said—and I'm paraphrasing—that it's easy to resist riches, fame, power, what's hard to resist, the most insidious of temptations, is the temptation to sainthood. And as I listened, swelling with pride because the Center had been able to guide these people back to meaningful lives, I reminded myself one more time that it was God, not Betty Ford, who had made these miracles. Inwardly, I thanked Him for including me.

When it came time for me to speak, I tried to say this. "I'm really proud of this Center," I said. "And I'm grateful for my own recovery, because with my recovery, I was able to help some other people come forward and address their own addictions. And I don't think there's anything as wonderful in life as being able to help someone else. But believe me, it's through the grace of God that I'm able to do it. It's not me, it's all you people put together, and a great staff, and my Higher Power that gives me the strength to try and keep it going. I love you all for that, and I thank you."

Winning a victory over drugs and alcohol doesn't mean you can rest on your laurels, you have to win again tomorrow. And I wished for all the people at the party that they would make it again tomorrow. And I hoped that they would wish the same for me.

What I remember best about that exultant evening is something said by a woman who told us she was forever getting herself into trouble. "But I just keep coming back," she said. "I just keep showing up for my life."

Showing up for life. Being blessed with the rebirth that recovery brings.

One day at a time.

AUTHORS' NOTE

No one needs to suffer alone and help is only a phone call away. Contact Alcoholics Anonymous, the National Council on Alcoholism, a clergyman or the local police department for help. Information about alcoholism or drug addiction can be found in your telephone book.